A HISTORY OF NEWPORT

The Guildhall. A sketch of one of the oldest buildings in the town. It has been proposed that it should house a museum of the town's history.

A History of
NEWPORT

Rob Prentice

Phillimore

1986

Published by
PHILLIMORE & CO. LTD.
Shopwyke Hall, Chichester, Sussex

ISBN 0 85033 568 X

Typeset in the United Kingdom by
Fidelity Processes - Selsey - Sussex

Printed and bound in Great Britain by
BIDDLES LTD.
Guildford, Surrey

CONTENTS

*This book is dedicated to
all historians of Newport,
past, present and future*

LIST OF PLATES

(between pages 80 and 81)

LIST OF TEXT ILLUSTRATIONS

Frontispiece: The Guildhall

ACKNOWLEDGEMENTS

A book like this is really a gathering-together of material from many different sources, and I am grateful to the many people who have discussed their different interests with me. I would like to thank the staffs of the County Record Office and County Library in Shrewsbury, and those of the County Record Office and William Salt Library in Stafford for their help in tracing Newport's early history. The staff of my local library kindly obtained various books for me which were not on their shelves.

I should like to thank Mrs. Ann Warner for her co-operation in obtaining photographs, and Mr. S. Brian Williams for giving me access to material at Liddle & Heane. Old advertisements which appeared in the *Newport and Market Drayton Advertiser* are reproduced by permission of Shropshire Weekly Newspapers Limited. I am particularly grateful to the following for permission to use items in their possession: Lady Wakeman, for a composite map of Church Aston and a map of Windmill Field; Shropshire County Record Office, for Telford's map of the canal past Newport; and the Curator in Aerial Photography, University of Cambridge, for the aerial photograph of the Iron Age Fort. I should also like to thank the late Rev. J. C. Hill and the Rev. Roy Hibbert for access to Church records.

Although those who helped me check the text, and those who typed it, wish to remain nameless, they also have my gratitude. I also wish to thank Dr. Frances Condick of Phillimore & Co., and Pamela Todd for compiling the index.

It has been said many times that I take my wife for granted. May I put on record my appreciation for all her help in my various ventures, and not the least, in this one.

ACKNOWLEDGEMENTS FOR ILLUSTRATIONS

I should like to thank the following for permission to use their photographs: Dan Arden, nos. 14 and 51; Mrs. Mary Burgess, nos. 32, 39, 47; R. H. Elkes, no. 24; Miss Hall, no. 22; the Reverend Hill, no. 15; Mrs. Horton, no. 27; Mrs. V. Jones, no. 29; Newport & District History Society, no. 1; Mrs. Sanders, no. 31; Roy Smallman, nos. 4, 5, 7, 8, 40 and 41; the Newport Literary Institute, no. 16; Local Studies Department, Shrewsbury Library, 43; the *Shropshire Star*, no. 53; Mrs. Tarry, no. 28; Brian Williams, no. 23. Other photographs are from the author's own collection.

I should also like to thank the following for permission to reproduce line drawings; first and foremost, I am most grateful to Stuart Timmins, who drew the frontispiece, nos. 5, 7, 10, 11, 13, 14, 15, 17, 19, 20, 22, 23, 27, 28, 31, 33, 37, 39, 41, 44, 50; no. 17 is taken from a photograph by Roy Smallman and is reproduced here by permission of Mr. Eastgate. In addition, thanks are due to David Roye Adam, no. 1; Newport Library, no. 16; Shropshire Archaeological Society, no. 39; and Brian Williams, no. 31. Other line drawings are by the author.

INTRODUCTION

I am delighted to have been asked to write the introduction to what is a most interesting and informative book about my local town. Interesting, because my family has been associated with Newport and the surrounding district for a very long time; informative, because I have learnt a good deal whilst reading my way through the following pages.

Newport is, of course, a town which has many similarities with many other market towns throughout England. Her history is no doubt every bit as fascinating as that of other towns, but the difference is that Newport has changed with the times. Light industries have been introduced here, in what has always been a predominantly agricultural area, but, nevertheless, the town has still kept its character. Many of the old buildings still stand, and indeed form the nucleus of the town. Many of the original families still live and work in the area, as they have done for countless years.

But let me detain you no longer: read on and enjoy this excellent book.

PREFACE

In 1958 Nikolaus Pevsner in *The Buildings of Shropshire* wrote:

> From the point of view of townscape, there is nothing better in North Shropshire than Newport. The town is really one long High Street wending its way gently to the Church and downhill to the Canal.

The whole of this High Street from Salter's Lane (Lower Bar) to Wellington Road (Upper Bar), including St Mary's Street, was designated as a conservation area in 1970 by the Shropshire County Council. It has a 'special architectural and historic interest, the character and appearance of which it is desirable to preserve and enhance'.

Looking at the town today, we see a wide High Street with a range of old narrow-fronted shops mingled with larger 20th-century self-service stores. Many of the buildings retain the character of town houses, with the roofs pitched from the street walls. There are also several indications that many of the premises had at one time been pubs or inns. We see some timber-framed houses, some red brick houses, and a red sandstone church. There are the remains of a railway station and a partially-filled-in canal.

Behind the main street there are wide car parks divided by narrow strips of land. Surrounding this central area, there are several large estates with owner-occupied houses, one large industrial complex, and one light industrial estate.

Looking at the town today, we start to ask questions: what changes have taken place over the years? Have recent newcomers radically altered the nature of the town, or are they unconsciously following a pattern which has evolved over the centuries?

It is necessary to understand how the past has affected the town in order to comprehend the present. This book is only the tip of the iceberg: there is much more to discover about Newport's history. If it encourages an interest in the town, it will have achieved its purpose — if anyone is tempted to take that interest further, and record further information about Newport for posterity, I would be delighted.

Rob Prentice
March, 1986

I

GLACIAL LAKE NEWPORT

The geological history of the area has had an important bearing on the formation and development of the town. The geological formation of the earth's crust caused an upthrust of high, comparatively soft mountains in parts of Britain which altered the climatic conditions caused by the prevailing winds. The rivers flowing from these mountains deposited sand and gravel into a shallow saline sea which covered the Midlands. As the climate was very warm and dry salt deposits were formed by evaporation, giving scattered salt beds. When drilling for an extra supply of water at Aqualate, near Newport, the Severn Trent Water Authority encountered such a salt deposit, and the operation had to be abandoned.

Other sand formations accumulated in the semi-arid conditions during the succeeding 80 million years as the Midlands became a flat, low-lying desert. The sand, as in any desert, was blown into large dunes. In our area the sandstone is a coarse-grained, pebbly reddish-brown with greenish patches, the rounded character of the grains suggesting that it originated as a wind-blown deposit. A good example of the bedding and nature of this sandstone can be seen in Edgmond quarry. The coarse-grained sand gives the maximum intergranular space capable of holding water.

A report in 1874 to the Newport Water Board states: 'The geological formation upon which the wells (Baddeleys) stand is the pebble beds of the new red sandstone, an admirable waterbearing sub-stratum, from which abundance of water may be obtained by carefully constructed wells and adits'. A report of a boring in 1889 at Walls Head in Church Aston states that: 'At 40 feet it has become more compact and harder, yielding 36,000 gallons per day. At 65 feet very soft red sandstone yielding 49 gallons per minute. At 70 feet soft red sandstone getting harder, yielding 25 gallons per minute. At 75 feet yielding 25 gallons per minute'. The report ends: 'The water is ideal for brewing'. This was well known to the inhabitants long before 1874, as we shall see later.

As the Triassic period passed, earth movements formed a wide syncline with its centre in what we now call the North Sea. As our area was on the rim of this basin, it had a marked effect on the soil here, clays and sandstone being deposited underlying the area around Newport. The red clay covering the Bunter sandstone makes a natural underground reservoir which, as we have seen, has been tapped by springs and bore-holes to supply the town with water. When a lump of this clay is broken it shows a

1

peculiar shell-shaped fracture. It also sets very hard on exposure to air in contrast to the red rock, some of which degenerates fairly quickly.

This clay was at one time thought to be Keuper marl, but it is now recognised that the absence of lime in its composition invalidates that description. This was borne out in James Loch's account in *The Improvements of the Estates of the Marquis of Stafford*: 'They [the farmers] also, until lately, hurt these cold lands by making use of a large quantity of a bad sort of red clay marl, which they dug out of every field. The effect produced was to increase the tenacity of the soil and to render it still less fit for the purpose of agriculture. The consequence of our prohibition has been that the tenants have applied themselves much more to the use of lime as a stimulant, which has repaid them, as might have been expected'.

There are numerous 'marlies' marked in fields in the district where the clay had been dug out. This practice was used throughout England, but with a different type of marl, as we shall see later. The Keuper clay can be found two or three feet down in several places in Newport, but does not seem to have any commercial use.

After the Triassic period there was no more alteration of the land forms in the Midlands until the top soils were modified during the ice age. These modifications resulted from the grinding action of the ice sheets, and the deposition of soil accumulations left when the ice melted. These resulted in various top soil types favouring different vegetation, and in some cases in the redistribution of surface water. This was instrumental in determining the original settlements, whose siting was dependent on the natural resources available for food, water, shelter and defence.

A series of ice ages began about three million years ago when the climate became much colder and caused huge glaciers to spread over most of Britain. These ice sheets brought large quantities of loose material from the mountains of Wales, Ireland and the Lake District. Another, coming south from Scotland, brought a different composition of detritus. In many parts of England these erratics, or misplaced rocks, can be found showing the tremendous carrying power of the slow-moving masses of ice. One such rock found at Broadhill had been used as a marker stone by earlier inhabitants. Between the colder periods the ice melted and, of course, our area regained its cover of vegetation only to have it wiped out again.

The retreat of the last ice age about 10,000 years ago is the one that is of most interest to us. As the climate grew warmer the front of the ice flow melted or retreated, and the enclosed accumulations were left *in situ*. The various names for these deposits — eskers, moraines or hog-backed pebble beds — need not concern us here except that at one time or another they were on hand to be used for road making, concrete, etc. The grinding movement of the glaciers as they slowly pressed forward pulverised some of the rocks, carrying the accumulation forward until, when the ice finally melted, a deposit of finely ground clay was left. This clay is very different in composition from the red clay which we have already mentioned.

The glacial clay is ideal for making bricks, tiles etc., several deposits in the district having been used for this purpose. The bricks for Forton Hall were made on the estate in 1668 and the timber used on it was felled on the estate. The house cost £90 to build.

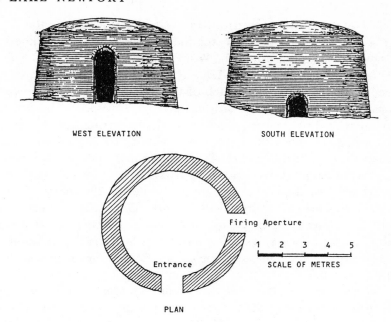

WEST ELEVATION   SOUTH ELEVATION

Firing Aperture

1   2   3   4   5

Entrance   SCALE OF METRES

PLAN

1. Old brick kiln, part of the Great Chatwell brickworks.

Another deposit on the Newport Marsh estate was the subject of a report by a Mr. G. Sidebottom in 1920:

CLAY — In the fields on each side of the railway (in the occupation of Mr. Hesbrook) we found a deposit of very rich clay and I believe, a large quantity. We have not tested for depth, but it covers a big area. This clay has been submitted to an expert of unquestionable reputation and I give you his exact words: 'One of the samples submitted is equal to the finest China clay from Devonshire and Cornwall, but is Terracotta not China. Either for casting or pressing, to make bricks of it would be sacrilege. A sample of clay has been fired and it is submitted for your inspection. You will notice it has a glaze, this is natural to the clay, only one firing is necessary, no glazing is required'.

This report was investigated by a firm from Stoke on Trent, but it was found that the depth was not sufficient to make it a commercial undertaking.

At the same time Mr. Sidebottom reported a find of silica sand.

SILICA SAND — It is known by different names but I prefer to call it Silica Sand. This is of very high quality and shows signs of being plentiful, it has great properties for cleaning and polishing and can be used for making glass, but of course the sand would have to be ground to a flour. This silica sand is also used as a moulding sand for the best quality work, it has been tested and found good for this purpose. Outcrops of red rock appear in various high spots, and in some lower places comes within a few inches of the surface. Not all the high ground is solid rock however, some being glacial drift or pebble beds.

There was, in the early part of this century, a pit for moulding sand on the site of what is now the Springfield industrial estate. This had been used by the engineering firms in the town.

Another benefit to the town came from the water left behind as the ice retreated. The melt water was impounded between the ice face and the surrounding higher land, the overflow originally escaping down the Worfe Valley and at Gnosall. This stretch of water is known to geologists as 'Glacial Lake Newport'. This lake, as the ice retreated beyond the Wrekin, joined a similar stretch of water known as Lake Lapworth, named after the geologist who calculated its position. Finding a low spot at Ironbridge the lake overflowed and, cutting through the softer rock, finally formed the Ironbridge Gorge. The river thus formed joined with the Stour and other tributaries to form the River Severn running into the Bristol Channel. The maximum extent of the lake can be seen from the map as being enclosed by land at approximately 300 feet O.D. As the gorge became deeper the level of the lake gradually fell, exposing the valley which runs from Gnosall down past Newport and the Weald Moors. This valley, having a gentle fall (25 feet in about five miles) was very slow in draining and the area as a whole, being fairly flat, resulted in meandering rivers, numerous pools in the hollows and a tendency to marsh and peat formation. One of these pools, fed by the Strine, stretched along the site of the present canal.

It is easy to accept that the rivers on either side of a range of hills like the Pennines will flow in opposite directions, but it is rather surprising to view the small land elevation at Gnosall and realise that it is the Midland watershed between the Trent flowing east into the North Sea and the Severn travelling west into the Irish Sea.

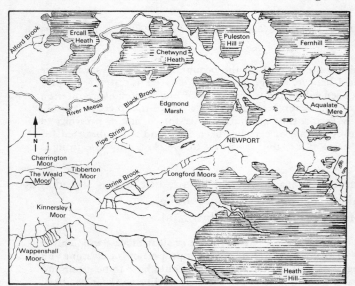

2. Pattern of drainage in the Newport area.

While the landforms have remained constant since the end of the ice ages, the slow change in the distribution of surface water has had a marked effect on the eventual settlement of the area. The now vanished Lake Newport was to play an important part in the siting of the town. Aqualate Mere, Meretown and Chetwynd Pools are, in fact, the last local remains of the lake. The prospect for early man in this area was the emergence of islands in a gradually receding lake, whose depth was determined by the level of the Severn. Newport is sited on a thin neck of land at 225 feet O.D. with the 200-foot contour just west of the canal bridge. About five miles farther down the Strine valley the drainage was blocked by the Weald Moors. The earliest description of these moors was given in 1673 by the Reverend George Plaxton. 'Wild moors so overgrown with rubbish, wood, alders, willows, salleys, thorns and the like that the inhabitants commonly hang bells around the necks of their cows. The moors seem to be nothing more than a composition of such sludge and refuse as the floods left on the ground when they drained away and yet this sediment is full three or four feet thick'. This description of the Weald Moors may well have applied to the whole valley in the time of Iron Age man, and even at the time of the advance of the Romans across the valley.

When the glaciers covered the area their effect stretched farther south giving a tundra-like landscape, frozen in the winter, but with trees and vegetation in the summer capable of supporting those animals which were adapted to such conditions. In the centuries between the various glaciations it may well have been the edge of the habitable world. As the land became clear of the ice, the plant colonisation of the land took place again, and eventually tree cover developed. When dry land is left derelict, grass and the small self-set plants are the first to show, followed by the stronger, higher-growing plants and grasses. The seeds carried by wind and birds take root where the

DATE	VEGETATION	FOREST COVER	CULTURES	CLIMATE		CONTINENT
2,000	ALDER – BIRCH – OAK (BEECH)	CLEARING OF FOREST BY MAN		Warmer and drier		
			NORMAN	SUB–ATLANTIC		
AD			ANGLO–SAXON	(cool and wet)		Roman Empire
BC			ROMANO–BRITISH			
			IRON–AGE		Increase in Peat	Alexander the Great
2,000	ALDER – MIXED OAK FOREST		BRONZE AGE	SUB–BOREAL (Drier)		David King of Jerusalem
			NEOLITHIC			Bronze Age Ur
4,000				ATLANTIC (Warm and Wet)	Peat Formation	Pyramid Age
6,000	HAZEL – PINE	FOREST	MESOLITHIC	BOREAL (Dry and Warmer)	Sea level rising. Britain separated from Continent	Stone – Age Jericho
	HAZEL – BIRCH PINE					
8,000	BIRCH			PRE–BOREAL (Less cold)	POST GLACIAL	

3. The geological post-glacial history of Britain.

soil is favourable to their growth, then the bush-type plants begin to show, followed by the trees pushing up to the sunlight.

Owing to the arid nature of the Triassic period no fossil evidence of life has been found here. In the peat formations of the post-glacial period, however, remains both of animals and man have been recovered. In the later glacial drifts in the Midlands remains of mammoth, woolly rhinoceros, musk ox, and reindeer have been found, also remains of the red deer and horns similar to those of the wild ox in the peat of the Weald Moor. When digging the Newport canal a set of horns similar to those of the gigantic Irish deer were unearthed.

The evidence of early settlements in the vicinity has been shown by the recent aerial photograph of the site of an Iron Age fort at Pave Lane. The estimate of the level of the glacial lake would mean that the sites of both Newport and Church Aston would originally have been under water, while the fort would have been above the shore line, which cuts the A41 at the *Wheatsheaf Inn* and, passing east of Pave Lane, went on through Stockton to Great Chatwell. A wooden dug-out canoe was also found there. At Wall Farm near Tibberton there is evidence of another fort, while at Adeney a bronze axe head and bronze crotal bell have been found. The finding at Puleston of another boat, and the existence, recorded in the Domesday Book, of two fish ponds, would suggest at least a fishing community. Mr. George Luff says in his article on Monolithic Man (*Shropshire Archaeological Society*) 'Among the meres and marshes of North Shropshire men had their dwellings behind reeds and willows on low-lying and difficult-to-approach islands'. The tools and habitations of Iron Age man were mainly perishable and it is only by the chance discovery of stone, metal or unusually well-preserved artifacts of other kinds which give clues to the lifestyle of our early ancestors.

The formation in 1982 of the Newport and District History Society has brought together some of these clues. The paradox is that modern research has brought as many questions as answers. It seems that some previously-held beliefs are being modified and, in some instances, rewritten. Study of place names, aerial photographs and even metal detectors are uncovering secrets hidden for centuries. The excavations for the Newport bypass might have given us an opportunity of reassessing the conventional view of early

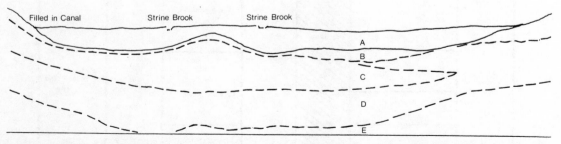

ISLINGTON   STAFFORD ROAD

4. The geology of Newport Pool: A, clayey sand and fibrous peat; B, silt and clay; C, fine sand and clayey silt; D, medium sand and gravel; E, completely weathered sandstone. Compiled from observations made during the construction of the by-pass.

Newport; unfortunately it was impossible for researchers to be there when the earth-moving was done. Nevertheless, a scattering of calcined stones might suggest a communal fireplace used by early man to heat his cooking water.

Although a complete picture of the early occupation in this area will not emerge for many years, we can imagine man adapting to an inhospitable setting. It also gives us a picture of the land in the marsh encountered by the Romans when they built their highway from *Penocrucium* (Penkridge) to *Mediolanum* (Whitchurch).

5. Early man with coracle.

II

VASTA REGALIS

Vasta Regalis (Royal Forest) or the Wrekin Forest were two names given to this area. This was not exactly a forest as we use the word today, but land used by the king and his nobles for hunting, and it was necessary to obtain permission before using it for other purposes. The name does give us some idea of the type of land surrounding the future town.

We shall see the relationship of the early fishing settlement to the development of the town in a later chapter, but the legacy to the town of the 400 years of the Roman occupation of Britain is in the road on which Newport stands. Looking at a map of Roman Britain we see only the main routes designated, similar to our 'M' system, joining areas or towns of importance. These roads were constructed for the fast movement of the legions into a conquered country, and for the export of its wealth back to Rome. Their method of planning the route was to fix an objective on forward high points by which means they were able to survey the alignment before hacking and pushing their way through the forest cover. In marshy ground they used a wattled base of brushwood before laying the stone base and overlay.

The road which first affected our town ran in an almost direct northwesterly direction from *Penocrucium* on Watling Street, three miles SSW of Penkridge, to *Mediolanum*, modern Whitchurch. Thomas Codrington, in *Roman Roads in Britain*, describes a highway 'of very near a straight line from Stretton near Gailey north-east to the Longnor Brook where the present road turns north to cross the brook by Stoneyford Bridge, disappears then reappears in two sections immediately north-east of Aqualate Mere, and again between Weston-Jones and Hinstock. Taking a line north-east from Stoneyford Bridge, south-east of Little Onn and north-east of High Onn Hill brings us to Wilbrighton. If we take the changes in direction on the high points, the line of the suggested road to Hinstock is no more than half a mile out of a straight line'. The part that is of interest to us is the probable route across the valley from Wilbrighton to Hinstock.

A trial trench dug in 1938 by the Old Stafford Society at a point near David's Pits Covert (Aqualate), on a stretch marked as 'uncertain' on the Ordnance Survey map, uncovered evidence of a gravelled road 15 feet wide in a field which appeared never to have been ploughed. I remember breaking a plough point on a headland at Wharton Grange (two and three-quarter miles to the north-west of Newport) on

8

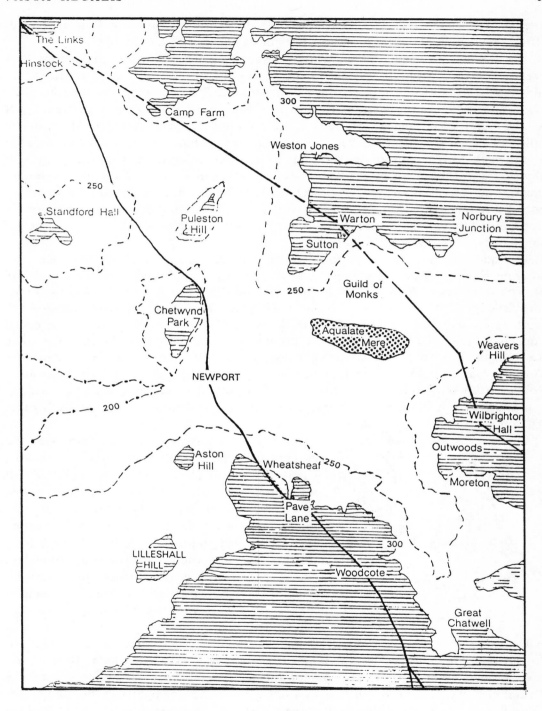

6. Glacial Lake Newport and the Roman road network.

unexpectedly large gravel. This headland is dead in line with the Roman road to Camp Farm. A recent excavation near Hinstock tallies with these findings.

The Romans reached Wall on Watling Street in A.D. 43 and this road must have been made soon after. It was called the 'Longford', probably a good comment on the state of the valley. Looking from Wilbrighton the Romans must have seen Aqualate Mere, and close on the west of it, Newport Mere, a pool more than a mile long. It would therefore be logical for them to take the route east of Aqualate Mere. In the valley this road is as near the 250 foot contour as possible, and no doubt follows what was then the driest land in a straight line to the Roman objective. Whether or not that objective was Chester or North Wales does not concern us here. Codrington describes the Watling Street from Stretton to Oakengates as no more than 200 yards out of line at any one time. Stukely says it was: 'laid very broad and deep with gravel not yet worn out where it goes over common and moors and was raised to a good height above the soil' (*Iterarium Curiosum*):

The question now arises as to why the Ordnance maps of 1900 name the road entering Newport from Pave Lane as a 'Roman Road' and leaving at Chetwynd End as 'The Longford'. 'At Stamford Bridge over the River Meese a road called the Longford is entered for eight miles between Hinstock and Bletchley. It was called the Lonford in the time of Henry III. In a repair of the road in 1319 it was called Longeford' (Eyton). Why has this road become a regular route over the centuries while the original Roman road has virtually disappeared? We have seen the reasons why Newport was bypassed in the first instance. Considering that there have been more Roman artifacts found at Wilbrighton than Newport, it would suggest that the second road must have had a greater advantage over the original road and eventually became the dominant route.

7. Roman legionaries

Geographers always ask 'did the road make the settlement or the settlement the road?' Newport, as it was to become, had a plentiful supply of fish and game, wells of good water, a ford across the valley, and it was a day's journey from a Roman settlement. Could it have been a resting place on a north-south trade route? The northern limit for vine cultivation is a July average of 66° F. I have eaten grapes grown outside on a western-facing wall in Newport. Did a retired legionnaire make a supply of wine for his compatriots who disliked British ale?

There are several suggestions of Roman occupation, which have to be verified, in the surrounding countryside, but it was land over 200 feet O.D. which attracted the next invaders from Europe. The Angles and Saxons moved into the area, using the natural clearings, and making others by stock grazing and tree felling, settled the higher ground. By 1086 we find these settlements described as being in existence in Edward the Confessor's time, and they were probably there before that.

The natural clearings, fertility of the soil, supply of water, and the wood for building and fuel, would determine the size of the original settlement. Depending on the ability of the soil to recover its fertility it was farmed on the two or three field system, i.e. one field was left fallow either every other year or one in three. The main draught animal was the ox, eight making up a plough team which, on average soil, was supposed to plough one acre a day. On most of the Edgmond land they could manage that, although on some of the stronger clay soils their furlong might be a little shorter. The types of horses in common use were not suited for heavy use on the farm. The ox, although slower, could live on much rougher food and hay than the horses, and yet do

the heavy work much better. The fields were cultivated in the strip system. This was still operating in Church Aston in 1680, and was certainly in use in Newport when the waterpieces were brought into agricultural use in 1309.

By A.D. 900 the main settlement here was Edgmond, with a subsidiary farming community at Church Aston. At Edgmond they had suitable land for crop farming, especially for barley. The woodland and moors would be used for grazing, and the valley could be used for the summer grazing of cattle and horses. Owing to the danger of liver fluke and foot rot, the sheep would have to be kept off the wet ground and grazed on the moorland.

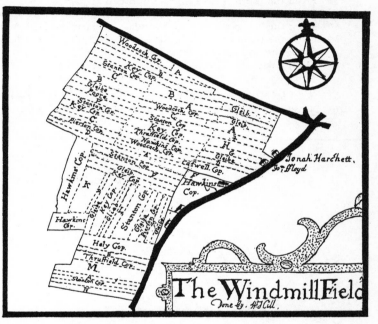

8. From a map drawn by William Hill, 1680, showing the strip system in the Windmill Field: A. Robert Woodcock; B. John Fleming; C. John Buckley; D. Christopher Casswell; E. Richard Shelson; F. John Liolm; G. John Hois; H. John Hatchett; I. Abraham Roc; K. John Kinsey; L. Rob. Davis; M. Thomas Smith; N. Will. Gery.

Newport did not yet exist as a named settlement. The first charter mentioning this area was granted in 963 by King Edgar to a thegn named Wulfric: '. . . a small portion of land, namely six hides, in the province of the Wrekin settlers, in two places — *Plesc* and *Easton*'. Easton is now called Church Aston and lies to the east of Edgmond, the parent church.

The boundary is described in Birch's *Cartularium Saxonicus* no. 1119. Owing to many changes the landmarks are now missing.

1 First to Diowic's path (*now Pave Lane*)
2 To the boundary of the Lil-settlers (*north boundary of Lilleshall*)
3 Along the brook to Eoata's ford (*where the old railway crosses the Wellington Road*)

4   From Eoata's ford to the great alder tree

5   From the alder to the great dyke (*Old English for 'ditch'*)

6   From the dyke to the Hoar Valley (*probably Longford Bottoms*)

7   From the Hoar Valley to the deep moor (*Moorfield House and Moorfield Lane show the survival in this feature in place-names*)

8   Along the middle of the moor to Aeslic's ford (*the construction of the canal and other developments have disturbed some of the other landmarks*)

9   From Aeslic's ford along the moor to the boundary of the religious community (*the boundary now matches that of Newport*)

10 From the boundary of the religious community to the three dykes

11 From the dykes to the tall thorn tree

12 From the thorn tree to the gap in the dyke

13 From the gap in the dyke to the broad rean (*furrow or open draining ditch*)

14 From the broad rean to the boundary sike (*rivulet at Parson's Barn*)

15 From the boundary sike to the boundary dyke (*county boundary along the Strine*)

16 Along the boundary dyke to Wiggerd's Tree

17 From Wiggerd's Tree again to Diowic's path

This corresponds closely with the present combined boundaries of Church Aston and Newport. Strangely, Newport Pool is not mentioned, but was probably in the holding of Edgmond and Chetwynd and it was only necessary to mention the marshy ground surrounding the southerly edge of it. The monastic settlement was probably placed to take advantage of the fishing in the Pool.

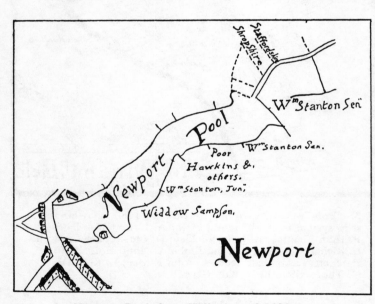

9. Newport Pool, from Hill's map of 1680.

The many watercourses, both natural and man-made, give us some idea of the continuing wet state of the land. The two fords mentioned show how important these places were, probably where the underlying sandstone appeared near the surface.

In *The Changing Climate*, H. H. Lamb says that 'in the year 1000 one of the warmest and most favourable climatic phases in historical times set in. With the summers dry and sunny, and the winters mild it helped the immigration of the Scandinavians. The increase in the population meant more land clearance under the plough to produce food'. Many changes took place in the first half of the century as the settlements grew; the formation of shires and hundreds; the influence of the church both in ecclesiastical and secular law increased; the growth of towns and importation of foreign goods both increased.

After 25 years' rule by Danish kings came the reign of Edward the Confessor who, although having Norman customs at court, still kept the Saxon style of government and lifestyle in the country. A picture of life in our area can be found in Domesday Book:

> Leuuin Cilt held Edmundene in King Edward's [the Confessor] times with six Berewicks. Here are xiv hides geldable. In demesne are vi ox teams and xii neat herds, and one female serf, xxxiii villeins and viii boors, with ii frenchmen, had xi teams, and yet there might be xi teams more. Here is a mill with a fishery, pays 10s. The manor used to pay £14.

The six berewicks were Pickstock, Newport, Church Aston, Little Aston, Little Hales and Adeney. When we look at the position of Newport today, against its lowly record on the Saxon manor and indeed among its neighbouring manors, one is reminded of the story of Joseph among his brethren.

Comparing the number of villeins or villagers and geldable or taxable hides of the Edgmond manor with those of the surrounding manors, there seem to be more villeins than one would expect from the hides recorded. The *Local Historian's Encyclopaedia* defines a villein as 'a general term to describe an unfree tenant who had a share in the agricultural system of the manor. He was above the status of a slave but was assumed to be annexed to the lord's pension. His usual holding would be about 30 acres'. Unlike the villeins, artisans and craftsmen were seldom mentioned in Domesday Book, which was primarily a record of the tenure of property, so that taxes could be levied on them. The status of ownership held sway in Newport until the Commonalty began to take an active part in the conduct of the borough.

Looking at Edgmond manor in the Anglo-Saxon economy, in the light of later developments, the owner had:

1. Between Edgmond and Pickstock, good barley growing and sheep grazing land yielding wool for spinning and weaving.
2. Church Aston and Little Hales had land suitable for the traditional two- or three-field system, with Little Aston on glacial clay, good wheat-growing land.
3. Adeney, an island in a valley 'with good pasturage and yielding great quantities of hay, though much of it is of such a nature as to dry up a new milch cow, starve a horse, and yet feed an ox to admiration' (Plaxton, 1673).
4. Newport, with a pool giving fish and wild fowl, a mill driven from the run-off from the pool to grind the corn; plenty of rushes for rushlights, candles from the tallow from the animals; alders for tanning; (beeswax was used in making better quality candles for the 'big house'); osiers for basket making; hemp for cords; water for making good ale for the travellers on a trade route running north and south crossed by what is now the B5062/A518.

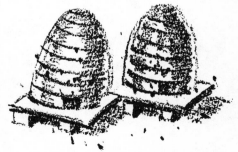

10. Beeskeps.

Professor W. G. Hoskins in *Fieldwork in History* says that 'Newport is silently included in its parent manor Edgmond at Domesday. In 1174 it was called Novus Burgos but the town was already over a hundred years old. Its name occurs on a coin of about 1050 as Nieweport'.

11. Monks gathering vegetables.

III

BEAU MARIS

We have seen the development of the area under the Iron Age, Roman and Saxon economies. England was now faced with another invasion, which would have far-reaching effects on the inhabitants of this settlement, and indeed on all England. William, Duke of Normandy, had been promised the English throne but, on the death of Edward the Confessor, Harold, Edward's brother-in-law, was appointed King. William landed in England with an army, defeated Harold and became William I of England, replacing the English landowners with the Norman nobility. Roger de Montgomery, William's nephew, was given most of Shropshire to act as a buffer against the Welsh. Roger thus became the earl of Shrewsbury and lord of the manors in the neighbourhood we are considering.

We have already seen the entry for Edgmond. It is worthwhile comparing it with the entries of the surrounding manors, especially as Newport did not rate a mention.

Longford

Thorold holds Longford from Earl Roger. Earl Edwin held it. 6 hides, with 4 outliers; they pay tax. In lordship 2 hides. 8 villagers have 3 ploughs. Two men-at-arms hold 4 hides from him. They have 3 ploughs and 4 ploughmen and 7 villagers, 3 smallholders and 1 rider with 3½ ploughs; a further 4 ploughs would be possible. A mill.

Value of the whole manor before 1066 £9; now 44s; he found it waste.

Chetwynd

Thorold also holds Chetwynd. Countess Godiva held it. 3 hides which pay tax. Land for 8 ploughs. In lordship 3; 6 ploughmen; 2 villagers and 3 smallholders with 1 plough. A priest. A mill with 2 fisheries which pay(s) 5s and 64 sticks of eels. A small wood.

Value before 1066, 25s; now 50s; he found it waste.

Kinnersley

Gerard holds Kynnersley from Earl Roger. Wilgrip held it. 1 hide which pays tax. Land for 4 ploughs. In lordship 1 plough; 3 slaves; 4 villagers and 3 smallholders with 2 ploughs.

Value before 1066, 21s; now 18s.

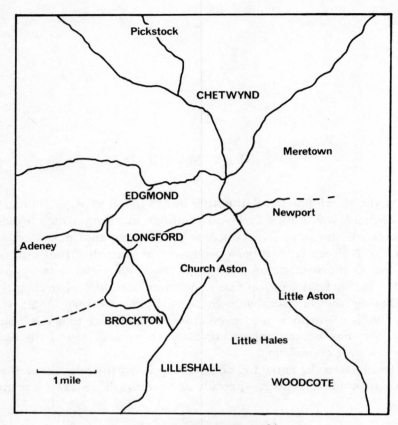

12. Manors and berewicks, 1086.

Cherrington

Wulfgeat held it. 3 hides which pay tax. Land for 6 ploughs. In lordship 1½; 3 ploughmen; 2 villagers and 3 smallholders with 1 plough.
Value before 1066, 23; now 22s; he found it waste.

Preston-on-the-Wealdmoors

Ralph holds Preston (upon the Weald Moors) from Earl Roger. Burrer held it. 1 hide which pays tax. Land for 4 ploughs. In lordship 1; 2 ploughmen; 3 villagers with 1 plough. Woodland, ½ league.
The value was 40s; now 20s.

Tibberton

Roger also holds Tibberton. Wulfgar held it. 5 hides which pay tax. In lordship 1 plough; 2 ploughmen; 4 smallholders with 1 plough; 7 more ploughs would be possible.
Value before 1066, 60; later it was waste; value now 10s.

Woodcote

> Robert also holds Woodcote, and Toki from him. Aelfric held it. 3 hides.... In lordship 1 plough; 2 ploughmen; 1 villager, 3 smallholders and 3 free men with 2 ploughs between them; a further 3 ploughs would be possible.
> The value was 20s; now 10s.

Brockton

> Richard holds ½ hide in Brockton from the Earl. Land for 1 plough. Aisil held it as one manor.
> 1 free man; he pays 16d.

These manors were held by men owing service to Earl Roger, but Lilleshall continued to be land held by the Church.

Lilleshall

> The Church itself held and holds Lilleshall. 10 hides.... In lordship 2 ploughs; 10 villagers, 5 smallholders and 3 Frenchmen who serve with 8 ploughs between them; a further 9 ploughs possible. 4 ploughmen. A mill, but it pays nothing; woodland, 1 league.
> Value before 1066 £6; now £4. Godbold the priest holds it.

Roger held Wellington, Tibberton and Edgmond himself.

Wellington

> Earl Edwin held it, with 5 outliers. 14 hides which pay tax. In lordship 6 ploughs; 12 ploughmen. 12 villagers and 8 smallholders with a priest have 9 ploughs; 9 other ploughs would be possible. A mill at 12s; 2 fisheries at 8s.
> Value before 1066 £20; now £18.

Edgmond was therefore designated a demesne manor where the owner kept the land for his own use and cultivation. He had his dwelling there and, when he was absent, his representative carried out the management of the estate with full powers.

Other neighbouring manors within the Newport district which later lost their importance relative to Newport were:

Meretown

A mill paid a rent of 3/– and 4,000 eels.

This was presumably a product of Aqualate Mere. There is no other mention of a pool in Staffordshire.

Sambrook

> Wulfgar held it. 1½ hides. Land for 7 ploughs. A man-at-arms holds from him; he has 1 plough. 5 smallholders with 2 ploughs. 1 mill which pays 64d.
> Value before 1066, 45s; now 16s; he found it waste.

Hinstock

> Saxfrid holds from him. Algar held it. 2½ hides which pay tax. Land for 5 ploughs. In lordship 1; 2 ploughmen; 1 smallholder. Woodland, 1 league.
> The value was 40s; now 8s.

Buttery

> Thorketel held it. 1 hide which pays tax. Land for 2 ploughs. 3 oxen only.
> The value was 6s; now 2s.

Isombridge

> Ralph holds Isombridge from Earl Roger. Ulf held it. 2 hides which pay tax. Land for 4 ploughs. In lordship 1; 2 ploughmen; 4 villagers and 3 smallholders with 2 ploughs. A mill which pays 3 packloads of corn. 1 man-at-arms has ½ hide of this land.
> The value was and is 20s.

Great Bolas was a part of the manor of Isombridge as Newport was of Edgmond. Later in the organisation of the hundreds, both Great Bolas and Newport were recognised as parishes in their own right.

Many things can be deduced from the Domesday information. The first feature is that the manors from Tibberton down the north side of the valley were described as 'waste', giving very low incomes. Secondly, the two manors reserved by Roger for his own use (Wellington and Edgmond) had been wealthy holdings in Saxon times, and thirdly, that the value of the manor of Edgmond had increased from £14 to fifteen pounds.

The Norman lords were well aware of the commercial value of their estates. One of the assets of the Edgmond estate was the berewick with the fishery, Bois Maris or Beau Maris.

It is difficult today to appreciate how important a plentiful supply of fish was in the economy of the Middle Ages. The church had ordered that no meat was to be eaten on specified fast days, including every Wednesday and Friday; thus fish, as a substitute, was in great demand. A special officer was in charge of the *vivary* or fishponds. The first known was one Reiner de Novo Burgo. In 1100 he was succeeded by his son Alexander Piscator (or 'fisherman') who was of sufficient importance to become a burgess in Shrewsbury.

In the 30 years of Earl Roger's control a thriving, if small, settlement developed on the site of the future town of Newport. When Earl Roger died he was succeeded by his son Hugh. When Hugh was killed in a hunting accident his elder brother Robert de Bellême, who had inherited considerable estates in Normandy from his mother, became the new earl. After the Conqueror's death his sons quarrelled over his inheritance. William's eldest son, Robert Duke of Normandy conspired with certain of the Norman nobles to dethrone his brother Henry I of England, but was defeated. One of the nobles who supported him was Robert de Bellême, earl of Shrewsbury.

Henry chose his time carefully in preparing a case to impeach Robert de Bellême, but eventually summoned him to appear at court. This Robert refused to do and garrisoned his castles. Henry took the field with his army, captured the castles one by one until he besieged Shrewsbury, held by Robert himself. He eventually surrendered and was banished from the Kingdom. Henry appropriated Robert's estates and thus Edgmond became a demesne manor of the King: and so New Borough (Newport) was born.

The king was a shrewd businessman, looking for the extra taxes to be raised from the growth of trade in the nation. He realised the advantages of creating market towns, not only to stimulate trade, but to regulate the buying and selling of goods under government protection. A system of tolls was charged throughout the kingdom, such as:

Murage: Toll for every cart or horse coming laden into a city for the repairs of its walls.

Pannage: Toll for pasturage of cattle in woods, feeding on acorns, masts for hogs, etc.

Pontage: Toll for maintaining bridges.

Piccage: Toll in fairs for breaking ground to set up stalls or standings.

Stallage: Toll for pitching stalls in fairs or markets without breaking ground.

The markets were spaced 10 to 15 miles apart to allow the farmers to get their produce to and from market in the best condition. A minimum of ten men were allowed burgages, or plots of land, on which to develop trading. These men were known as 'burgesses'. In Newport they held the town under the jurisdiction of the lord of the manor and rented their burgages to tradespeople.

Although the burgesses claimed to have a charter from Henry I's reign, no written record of it has been found, and it was in any case necessary to obtain renewal of charters from succeeding sovereigns. In 1163 Henry II, while at Brewood, confirmed in writing the rights and liberties of New Borough:

> Henry, King of England and Duke of Normandy and Aquitaine and Count of Anjou. To the Sheriff and all his ministers of Shropshire. Know ye that I have granted to my Burgesses of New Borough all their liberties and good customs as they the better and more fully possessed them in the time of King Henry my Grandfather, and accordingly, on this account I prohibit everyone from doing injury or contempt therefore, and if anyone shall injure them in their liberties and their customs or in any of them, you shall without delay do them justice. Witnessed therof Geoffrey Archdeacon of Canterbury: John Cummins. At Brewood.

He also granted three virgates of land to Robert Penzun of Church Aston 'by service of providing two trusses of hay for the King's Chamber whenever he should sleep at Edgmond'. In return for the grant of the charter, the burgesses of Newport were required to convey fish from the vivary to the king's court, wherever it might be.

Newport thus became a town in its own right, separate from the manor of Edgmond, a settlement on a trade route, bounded on the west by the farming lands of Church Aston with a stretch of water along the northern boundary. On the east there was the common grazing land of Norbroom, running down to the water-logged marsh at the end of the pool. .

Taking into account what we have found of the peat deposits and the in-fillings along the valley, the pool must have been fairly extensive if not very deep. It would appear that the early Norman settlement stretched from the church along Victoria Park, divided by the marsh brook (now piped) where the tannery was situated. A later find of charred building beams suggested that the concentration of buildings, as the town grew, was between the church and Wellington Road.

As a stopping-place on a busy route, the wide space beyond the church now became the market place, enclosed by narrow burgage plots (narrow to give the maximum number of trading frontages), the land running in long strips back from the street. These can still be seen in the High Street today, together with their tall, narrow houses. The passages between the burgages are all on the north side, no one seems to know why. It was important to the burgesses to have as many rent-payers as possible on their property, as they were landowners, not necessarily residents in the town.

Like most market towns, Newport retained a rural atmosphere. There was a common for grazing, gardens and orchards, byres and pig styes. The function of a town like Newport was to give the local people an outlet for their produce and cash for rent, taxes and to buy manufactured goods, and, being on a main thoroughfare, service for travellers.

The manor and town organisations existed side by side under the same lord of the manor. In the demesne manor, the lord or his steward farmed the land with servants and the part-time help of his tenants. The steward was responsible for the overall management: he fixed the fines and collected the money. The lord would allow his tenants land on which to farm in return for specified days of work on the manor. He had absolute control over all the personnel on the estate, and no one was allowed to settle on, or to leave the manor without his permission. It was possible for suitable lads to acquire some education, if they were destined for the priesthood, but the father of such a boy had to pay a fine (13 shillings) for the loss to the manor of his son's earnings. If a woman wanted to marry 'off the manor' — a stranger from elsewhere — they had to pay *merchat* — half a ploughman's annual wage. Any unmarried woman caught in a compromising situation had to pay *leywrite* which was a fine of one month's income.

The town dweller was free from these manorial restrictions. If anyone leaving the manor managed to live in a town for a year and a day undetected, he was considered a free man. Obviously, this would only be possible for a skilled or semi-skilled artisan who would be acceptable for his skills to the businessmen in the town.

In the course of centuries, the church gradually took over the duties of the manor, the vestry becoming the local governing body. Once a year at Easter officials like the overseer of the poor, surveyor of the highways and constables were chosen by the vestry. The constables had very wide duties including upkeep of stocks and pounds; inspecting ale houses and suppressing gaming houses; apprenticing of pauper children; settlement or removal of itinerant strangers and beggars; welfare of the poor;

collecting county rates, supervising military arms and training militia; presenting the people who did not attend church regularly; convening parish meetings; and caring for the parish bull!

We shall see the varying changes in local government as time progresses and how the reorganisation of government on a national scale also had effects on the town.

The first association of the town with the name of Audley came in 1227. In a charter dated 22 July, Henry III granted the 'manor of Edgmundon cum Nova Burgo to Henry de Audley at the rent of one sore sparrowhawk payed yearly at the feast of St Michael'. Henry de Audley was a big landowner and one of King Henry's most powerful courtiers. He had helped him in many ways, and, as a mark of respect, he was given what was virtually the king's town. Twenty years later, James de Audley quitclaimed to the burgesses of Newborough 'that they shall not carry the fish of the vivary of Newborough any whither except within the boundaries of Shropshire', that is either to the king or de Audley. For the release from the original commitment, the burgesses paid five pounds.

The pool had played an important part both in the trade of the town and the recompense to the sovereign for the charter, but this release probably began the shrinkage of the original sheet of water. Perhaps the fish trade was becoming of less importance and the land which was uncovered became of more importance to the town. We will find references to The Flaggs, Waterpieces etc., at a later date.

A further grant in 1292 by Nicholas de Audley extended the land under the control of the burgesses towards the above-mentioned Watermeadows, granting

> free common pasture for all, and all manner of their cattle and animals, in a certain place on my lands which is called Brodmersh which lies between these boundaries, length from the Vill of NewBurgh to the ditch of Long Meadow, and in width from the open fields of Great Aston to Northbroom.

For this grant the burgesses paid 10 marks of silver and 20s. per annum, and it provided pasturage for cattle until it was enclosed in 1764. The word 'commonalty', as used here, will have an important meaning in the affairs of the town, as we shall see on future occasions.

Although the wide High Street was admirable for the weekly market, the need for a covered place for day to day commerce led Lord de Audley to make a further grant to the town of

> a certain place of land in the Vill of Newport containing in length, 40 feet, extending from the house of Richard de Blakelow against the wall of the churchyard against the highway, and in width, 30 feet from the aforesaid wall of the aforesaid churchyard against the cross erected for the soul of Roger de Puleston for 20s. of silver which the aforesaid Burgesses and their heirs, freely and quietly, well, honourably and hereditably, to build up the aforesaid place and to carry on all manner of trades and all other their affairs forever.

This gave them a place for merchandise and was later the site of the Booth Hall. The rent was three shillings of silver per annum. Unfortunately, the site was not to be so used 'forever', as we will see.

The position that Newport had now attained is shown in an entry in the tenure roll of the Bradford hundreds:

Nicholas de Audley holds the manor of Edgmond with its members, rendering yearly a mewed sparrowhawk. The said manor was a demesne manor of the King. William Eysseby holds Great Aston; the abbot of Crokesden holds Adeney; John de Hallis holds Little Hallis and the burgesses hold Newport as a free borough of the said Nicholas and here the said Nicholas has free court, and pleas of bloodshed, and hue and cry, and gallows, warren, market and fair, and these he has used.

The gallows were erected in the middle of the marsh on a spot called Gallows Bank.

The growth of the town and the increased trade began to put a strain on the water supply. Although the pressure in the artesian wells was enough to supply water at the level of the High Street, only the houses with their own wells benefited. A scheme was inaugurated to use the water from the Walls Head spring at Church Aston.

Know all men, present and future, that I, Richard Attebruggehend of Newport have given, granted and by this my present deed confirmed for me and my heirs to the Burgesses of Newport and to all the commonalty of the same power and license to open dig and place leaden pipes through the midst of my land so that the water of the spring, which is called Wodewall at the Vill of Newport may flow at pleasure. The aforesaid burgesses or successors shall give me and my heirs 2s. of silver when and as often as such work of amending or also of repairing shall happen. But for this gift, grant and my present deed of confirmation the aforesaid Burgesses have given me in hand 8s. in silver.
      Dated at Wodewalle on Monday the morrow of the apostles Peter and Paul in the second year of Edward son of King Edward (1309).

Four cisterns were constructed in the town, built below street level, one midway between Upper Bar and the market hall; one at the end of the market hall; one at the end of the Butter Cross; and one midway between the church and Lower Bar. Two

13. Boy at village pump.

things to note in this grant is the mention of 'commonalty', which would seem to indicate that a class of businessmen below the rank of burgess were taking an increasing share in the conduct of the town, and that expensive leaden pipes were used, indicating Newport's prosperity. The Walls Head spring was used until Baddeley's Well was developed to give the present supply.

We have noticed the shrinkage of the pool to make more land available: this land was then used to supply money for the upkeep of the water system.

In order to pay for the upkeep of these services, Nicholas de Audley quitclaimed to the burgesses certain lands 'in the waste of Calvercroft' the rent of which was to be used for expenses incurred in the supply of water. These lands became known as the 'waterpieces', 'lands and wastes within the metres of open field of Northbroom in the land and wastes of Calvercroft together with two little marshes lying next the Vill aforesaid with a certain lane to the same adjoining at all time of the year with the appurtenances'. This land was enclosed and let in small 'pieces of land'.

In 1315 Richard de Geydon gave a messuage he had to the town in aid of the water conduit. In 1317 John de Tornour gave two plots of waste, from a meadow called 'Algehmundesmedive', one of which was 'in Norbroom called Middlehit' for the same purpose.

The effect of the increase of traffic in the town was causing a deterioration in the upkeep of the streets. As each man was responsible for the frontage of his property, it was becoming a serious burden on the traders. In 1298 Lord de Audley had obtained letters patent, valid for three years, stating that dues on merchandise sold in the town would be payable in order to raise money for repairing the streets. In 1356 the burgesses obtained permission for the same purpose. These lists show the variety of goods which could be sold in the town. A bale of leather was taxed at threepence while one hundredweight of the skins of lamb, kids, hares, 'conies' (rabbits), foxes, cats and squirrels were a halfpenny. One hundredweight of *grisei operis* (a high quality grey cloth) fetched sixpence, linen cloth of Aylesham and *cendallo affortico* (silk) one penny and Irish cloth, Gaylesworth and worsted cloth a halfpenny. A load of meat paid one penny, a cart of corn a halfpenny, but a load of honey one penny, and a hundredweight of cheese or butter a farthing. Salmon was also taxed at a farthing, 12 lampreys or 1,000 herrings at one penny and a load of sea fish at a halfpenny, 'sherries allee' at a farthing, 2,000 'allee and cepary' (varieties of onions) at a halfpenny. Wood, coal and turves (peat) were also on the list which included 'a quarter of Wayde' at twopence. Timber, tin, brass, copper and lead were also taxed and as would be expected, horseshoes and nails.

Shropshire was the first shire named in a written record in 1006 as the area to which King Ethelred had fled from the Danes. For government purposes it had been divided into 'hundreds'. These hundreds, being defined on numbers of people or hides of land in cultivation, were flexible in area so that, although Shropshire was the largest landlocked shire in England, it was divided into only 15 hundreds, and did not exist as an administrative unit until early in the 11th century. In Saxon times Newport, a berewick, was in the hundred of Recordin, but in 1158 the name was changed to Bradford with these boundaries: 'gives on the North by Cheshire; on the East by Staffordshire and the hundreds of Brimstry; South by the franchise of Wenlock and the River Severn; West by the liberties of Shrewsbury, the hundreds of Pimhill and Flintshire'. This was in fact an amalgamation of the former hundreds of Recordin and Odonet.

The Newport division of the Bradford South hundred was composed of the parishes of Chetwynd, Great Bolas, Newport, Edgmond, Lonford, Kinnersley, Preston on the Wealdmoors, Lilleshall and Sherrifhales; the Petty Sessions were in Newport. In Saxon times Great Bolas and Newport were parts of manors, but the others were manors in their own right. The Saxon pattern of mother vills and daughter settlements, such as Edgmond and the berewicks, was changed by the establishment of market towns. Here we have an example of how a daughter settlement, Newport, could achieve complete independence from the mother settlement, Edgmond.

In the surrounding area, even in 1826, when Telford made his map of the Newport canal, Lilleshall, Longford, Chetwynd, Chetwynd Aston, Meretown and Forton were all named as townships. Newport was named as a town, but the surrounding area is labelled 'Newport township'. In Saxon times the freeman of the vill or township used to meet to make their own bye-laws at the town moot where they elected the headman or reeve, and the tithing man (one of ten) or constable to enforce the rules. The land-owner (the earl or his representative) administered justice, and this continued after the Conquest.

A system of travelling justices (Justices in Eyre) kept the central government in overall control. In 1176, when the justices visited Newport, they discovered three houses in Newport built in such a place or manner 'as they were in the nature of a purpresture' (squatters' houses) and were not protected by the town's usual dues of £12 2s. 6d. Three shillings were added to the dues. The 'Vill of Novus Burgos' and Nicholas de Pulcer were each fined two marks for harbouring a person excommunicated by the church, together with William de Novo Burgo and Adiven Telimes who were also fined forty shillings.

At the assizes in 1203 Newport was represented by 12 jurors because it was 'extra hundredal' and 'kept its own Pleas of the Crown'. There is a mention in 1252 of 'the Hundred Court of Novus Burgos'. The Lord Bailiff granted the burgesses 'free from appearing at Small Courts and on appeal only at Leets'.

In 1255 at an Inquisition of the hundred 12 jurors gave account of the joint manors of Edgmond and Newport. They valued the vill and mill at Newport at £13 3s. 8d. annually, the manor of Edgmond at £7 19s. 6d. annually, the tallage of Newport at 36 marks, and the tallage of Edgmond at 50 marks. One mark was worth two-thirds of one pound.

The main ambition of the growing towns was to manage their own affairs, especially financially. In 1292 there is a record of the burgesses claiming that they had the right to assize bread and ale in relation to the local price of corn and malt, that they had a merchants' guild, and that they had exercised their franchises 'from time whereof memory was not'. (The translation of this quotation is usually given as 'bread and beer' but as hops, the ingredient which distinguishes beer from ale, were not grown in this country until early in the 14th century, the beverage must have been ale.) Local authorities appointed aletasters to examine bread and ale for quantity and quality.

As Newport developed, the owners of the various businesses began to have more influence in conducting the affairs of the town but were not felt to have had the same status as the land-owning burgesses. We find them being referred to as 'the commonalty'. The first mention of this phrase was in 1306 when 'the Consent by the Commonalty of Newport to come before the Bailiffs of the Lord to take an Oath to answer concerning articles touching the great Court'.

The town became increasingly prosperous. In 1160 the tax due to the king amounted to one pound. In the following year it had risen to £2 13s. 4d. After 200 years the success of the town may be seen in the following comparison of burgage rents with market tolls.

	Year	Burgage and other rents	Tolls at fair and markets	Profits of Justices
Newport	1316–17	£14 1s. 0d.	£7 6s. 0d.	£5 13s. 0d.
Llandovery	1316–17	£3 18s. 0d.	£4 13s. 4d.	£2 0s. 0d.

If the burgage rents were each one shilling, then this would suppose a maximum of 81 burgages. The market was prosperous enough to contribute nearly twice as much in income. The profits of the Justices denote the standing that Newport held in the local government.

The country in the vicinity of the Wrekin called '*Vasta Regalis*' or the Royal Forest had long been designated the king's domain, used for hunting, with penalties against trespass. Even in natural clearings, no building or farming was allowed, except under licence. This land had been gradually encroached upon and finally in 1300 some areas were 'disafforested'. In this area were 'the boscs and plain of Little Hales, Woodcote, the Abbey of Lilishull, the vills of Lilishull, Lonford, Egemund and one half of Novus Burgos'. This may have been the half not previously granted under the king's charter, and would have allowed building to take place on the land east of the town.

The acquisition of land by the burgesses was again seen in 1313 when they rendered to Lord de Audley four silver shillings at two terms of the year, giving 10 marks of silver in hand, 'the said Nicholas quitclaimed all the rights and claims which he had in the land and wastes within the metes of the open field of Northbroom together with two little marshes lying next to the Vill aforesaid with a certain land to the same adjoining'. This land, now lying between the recently built Norbroom housing estate and the bypass, is being scheduled as a nature reserve.

Although in 1325 the vivary was mentioned in an inquisition ('a water mill and a vivary') it is obvious that all the pieces of land east of the town were gradually becoming less marshy and more amenable to agriculture. There must have been farmers either residing in the town or on farms just outside it, for in 1356 James de Audley, lord of Ruge Chasteil (Hawkestone) and of Helagh (Staffordshire) 'received of Roger Rondulf and William Longe, our farmers of Newport £7 3s. 4d.' The Rondulf family had a long association with the town as burgesses. In 1278 the third Robert de Woodcote died and his son alienated the Woodcote estate to William Rondulf of Newport.

In that same year James de Audley was in France. He had raised four footmen from Newport to fight beside the Black Prince against the French. At Poitiers he 'broke through the French Army and caused much slaughter that day to the enemy'. He was severely wounded in the body, head and face and after the battle the Prince recompensed his services by 'retaining you henceforward as my Knight, with five hundred marcs of yearly revenue'. James, remembering the four squires who had supported him throughout the battle, gave them the 500 marcs. When the Black Prince heard of this, and the reason for it, he confirmed the original gift to James and insisted that he accepted 'six hundred marcs on the same terms and conditions as the former gift'. James was in fact the third James de Audley (lord of the manor of Newport), and was also lord of the manor of Ford, Shropshire. He died without issue in 1392 at the age of 71.

14. Timber-framed houses.

IV

NEW BOROUGH

There seems to be no great change in the town during the next 300 years especially in the rate of its growth. Although the town had control of its own affairs, most of the indentures of the lords of the manors link Edgmond and Newport together, showing that it was still seen as part of an agricultural area. The town was, however, involved in matters of a wider significance which eventually affected the pattern of the community.

On the death of the third Sir James de Audley in 1392, the manor was divided between Lord Foulk Fitzwarren, Sir John Hillary and Sir John Toucher who had married Joan de Audley. Their grandchild, John Toucher Lord de Audley, was born in 1400 and summoned to parliament in 1421. His second marriage was to Eleanor, natural daughter of Lady Constance Plantagenet and the Duke of York, on whose death the other heirs preferred a Bill of Parliament (1431) which declared Eleanor Lady Audley to be the offspring of 'pretended espousals' and entitled to no part of the duke's estates. This gave the Audleys a grievance against York and, not surprisingly, when he tried to take the throne, the Audleys were on the Lancastrian side. In 1459 Lord de Audley was summoned by Queen Margaret to stop the advance of the Yorkist army of 5,000 men who were trying to reach the Duke of York, stationed at Ludlow. De Audley raised troops from his three castles at Heleigh, Hawkestone and Newhall, and from his manors, including Newport, and established his forces at Bloreheath, near Market Drayton, on Sunday 23 September 1459 while the Queen stayed in Eccleshall Castle with 2,000 men.

The earl of Salisbury, the Yorkist commander, greatly outnumbered, withdrew the pikemen in the centre of his line and tempted de Audley into a charge which suffered severely from the Yorkist archers on the flanks. The longbow was a formidable weapon, able to drive through the protective armour of the day, and an archer was supposed to be able to get his sixth arrow in the air before the first one landed. Faced with crossing a brook and a steep climb up the opposite bank, de Audley rallied his forces and charged again, only to be killed in the assault. His second in command, Lord Dudley, then charged but 500 of his men, seeing how the battle was going, changed sides and fought for the Yorkists, so the battle was lost. It had lasted all afternoon and the pursuit continued until 'seven at the bell in the morning'.

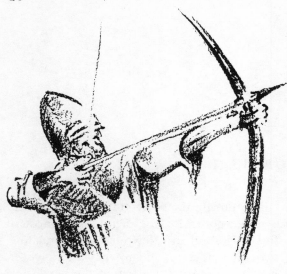

15. Longbowman.

Salisbury, fearing a counter-attack from Eccleshall, deputised a local monk to fire guns all night to cover his retreat to Market Drayton. Although there is no record of artillery or guns being used in the fighting, as gunpowder was still a novelty then, the effect of the noise did all that was required. Whether or not Salisbury advanced to Ludlow via Shrewsbury, or through Newport and Bridgnorth, there is no record.

Lord de Audley was buried at Darley Abbey, Derbyshire. His son, Roger, by Eleanor, eventually turned to the side of York, later rebelled against Henry VII, and was beheaded in 1497. Roger's son son was restored to the title but the family fortunes declined from then on.

In 1508 Anne, daughter of Thomas Audley, who had married George Twynnho, alienated a moiety of the manor of Newport to her son who disposed of it to Sir Thomas Lodge, citizen and alderman of London. He, in 1558, alienated the estate to Robert Barnfield, whose heir, Richard, had licence to alienate to Walter Leveson of Lilleshall a moiety of the manor of Newport viz. '20 messuages, 10 lofts, 20 gardens, 20 orchards, 100 acres of land, 40 acres of meadows, 300 acres of pastures and 20s. rent with appurtenances, one water mill, View of Frank Pledge, held in capite from the Queen'. No fishery is mentioned although it may have been in another moiety. Walter Leveson was seized of 32 manors in Shropshire and Staffordshire, including Newport. In his will he specified that in default of issue his estates should pass to William Gower, provided he assumed the surname 'Leveson'. In 1689 Sir William Leveson Gower married Lady Jane Granville, thus the moiety of the manor of Newport eventually came to George Granville William Sutherland Leveson Gower, the Duke of Sutherland, lord of the manor of Newport.

It does not seem that the lords of the manor were in the habit of residing in Newport, for in 1421 the manor house had become so ruinous as to be valued at nil per annum, but still at 13s. 4d. rent of assize. The situation of the manor house is not known, but on the Ordnance map of 1881 a moat is shown on the south side of the Wellington Road. Many large country houses have a 'ha-ha' or concealed ditch surrounding them. This moat may have been the remnant of one of those, perhaps the stones of the house had been carted away to be used elsewhere.

The part that the church has played in the development of English settlements has been an important one. The buildings themselves have always been landmarks, and their purpose central to British life. And as we have seen, in later centuries the vestry controlled the secular as well as the moral conduct of the parishioners. Another important role usually left to the clergy was that of education.

In Saxon times there was a religious community here, although nothing is known of it at the moment. With the coming of the Normans, however, we know that a church was established in the town, taking its part in the conduct of local affairs. National trends also had an influence on the town. As the economy of the nation expanded the increase in trade meant a need for more people to be educated for administration.

Many successful London merchants and manufacturers bought themselves estates; others invested their money in the church. One of those was Thomas Draper, a native of Newport and, at one time, a member of the household of the duke of Gloucester. In 1452 he bought the church in Newport from the abbot of Shrewsbury by permission of Henry VI. A chapel was endowed as a chantry to sing masses 'for the furthering of God's worship and the perpetual help-
ing of the Souls of the Faithful Departed'. This chantry of the Virgin gave St Mary's Street its name. In 1455 Pope Eugenius IV, on the petition of Henry VI and Humphrey, Duke of Gloucester, granted an indulgence to the persons who 'on the Feast of the Assumption of the Blessed Virgin Mary shall visit and give alms to the Chapel of St Mary the Virgin in the Parish Church of Newport'.

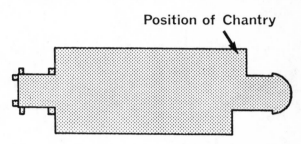

Position of Chantry

16. Sketch of the church in 1825, showing the position of the chantry.

Draper also founded the College of St Mary as part of his endowment. A '*custos*' and four assistant chaplains had the care of the church until 1491 when Roger Salter became the priest in charge.

The school in the town must have been in constant use as we find that the English School in Newport was certified in 1548 to have been kept by Richard Robins, one of the fellows of the college. This information was given in order to qualify for Grammar School status under a statute of Edward VI, which said that 'provided that in every place where a guild or fraternity, by the foundation ordained or first institution thereof should, or ought to have kept a Grammar School and had done so since the Feast of St Michael the Archangel, then the institution should be a Grammar School'.

Newport was fortunate during the troubled years when the college and chantry schools, like the monasteries, were dissolved by Henry VIII. The deacons of the original schools were allowed to continue teaching if they so wished. The chantry and college lands were bought by a John Cupper and Richard Trevor at the dissolution of the monasteries, but by the order of the duke of Northumberland, chief of the Council of State in 1552, 'all persons holding Chantry land at the commencement of the reign of Edward VI should restore it to the Crown'. The name English School, of course, meant that the English tongue was spoken and taught alongside Latin. This school continued through the years in the Booth Hall.

In 1656 William Adams founded the Grammar School with two almshouses in the grounds. William Adams was born in Newport in 1598 and attended the English School.

17. William Adams' crest.

Later he went to London as an apprentice, and became a member of the Worshipful Company of Haberdashers. Having acquired a considerable fortune he used it to benefit Newport in many ways. In his will, made 'the seven and twentieth day of November in the year of Christ' 1656 the following passage occurs:

> Forasmuch as it is being in my experience found that the Booth Hall where the school for the said Town was formerly held was very ill convenient, if not hurtful, both for the Town Schoolmaster and scholars, the said Wm Adams for a further manifestation of his goodwill and pious Institution of his redress here purchase ...

Here he sets out the burgages purchased and the houses in which he founded the Adams Grammar School.

Adams negotiated with Oliver Cromwell and the letters patent for the foundation of the Grammar School were granted by him. The headmaster of Shrewsbury School, whom Adams wanted as his headmaster, disagreed with Cromwell and left Shrewsbury, taking all the school money with him. After a sojourn at Wem he was installed at Newport, presumably, however, with Cromwell's permission. The following are excerpts from the settlement:

> This indenture made between Wm Adams of the City of London Esq. of the one part and the Master and four Wardens of the Fraternity of the Art of Mystery of Haberdashers in the City of London Governors of the possessions and Revenue of the Free Grammar School of Newport in the County of Salop of the foundation of Wm Adams of the other part ... Wm Adams hath willed, granted and ordained that forever thereafter there be and should be in the said Town of Newport in the County of Salop one free Grammar School for Education and Instruction of Children and young ... called the Free Grammar School of the foundation of Wm Adams and that one Master and one Usher be there forever for the better effecting of the pious Intention of him the said Wm Adams that the Master and four Wardens of the Fraternity of Haberdashers should be called Governors ... and shall pay out of rent twenty pounds of lawful money of England to such Godly, Orthodox and learned Minister who shall forever weekly Catechise the said Scholars, Children and servants of the said town as shall for that purpose repair to the church aforesaid whereby they may know God and their duties towards Him and their Superiors.
> A yearly sum of Forty Pounds to such able and learned Schoolmaster who shall have been educated at one of the Universities of Oxford or Cambridge and hath there taken the Degree of

Master of Arts and is well read in the Greek and Latin tongues. He shall teach gratis and forever all such children of the Town of Newport as will repair there to learn Latin and Greek Tongue.

One other yearly sum of twenty pounds to one other able and learned scholar of Godly life and Conversion who shall have been educated at one of the Universities and taken the Degree Bachelor of Arts.

The sum of Twenty shillings to any other poor boy being a scholar to clean the said School-house with the seats, benches and desks thereto belonging (the Lord's Day excepted).

One other yearly sum of Twenty pounds like money for the maintenance at the Universities of four scholars to be sent to one of the Colleges of Oxford or Cambridge from the said free school.

The Grammar School foundation is typical of many which took place throughout England. The merchant class wanted a godly ministry to preach and also, by influencing the education of the poorer classes, by reading the Bible under direction, to encourage the spread of godliness. The gentry, also, especially the younger sons, wanted an education to fit them as 'men of affairs'.

The English School was not forgotten in Adams' will. He gave 'unto the Bayley of the Burgesses of Newport for maintenance of the English School usually kept in the Booth Hall all these two closes situated in Norbroom which I purchased, together with two parcels of land called Gamble byrches the rents for the maintenance of the English school being to the end the Children of the poorest people in Newport civil and honest demeanour may be taught there freely to read English'.

18. Newport Town Hall and Butter Cross in the late 19th century.

Also in Adams' will was '£550 in trust to build a Market House with a Town Hall over it according to a model and other directions by me provided. It shall be supported with pillars of Hard Stone which shall be or may be got in my land at Knighton and the building over them to be of brick and stone and timber. I conceive no fitter place than between the Height of the Pavement in the High Street, and the Height of the Pavement in St Mary's Street between the house usually called the sign of the Crown and Back House Lane'. It is probable the English School moved into the Market Hall, as later on the Marsh Trust used one of the rooms for a Sunday School. I can find no other record of the school until 1840, when it occupied premises at the corner of Wellington Road and Upper Bar.

It was necessary to get the foundation of the Grammar School recognised by Charles II after the Restoration; it is said to have cost Adams £1,000 to obtain the king's consent. Adams arranged that the foundation was under mortmain. As he had also bought land in Knighton to secure an income for the foundation it meant that this land was free from any dues to the government. As the covenant was under the great seal of Charles II, this land is free of county rates to this day.

Following the tradition of alms giving, a part of the medieval system of giving to the poor in church, William Adams also founded two almshouses, which are still in use today, in the grounds of the school.

This was in addition to a grant by the burgesses in 1446 to William Glover of a piece of land 'between the churchyard and the King's highway in breadth toward the north between two stiles in the said churchyard on condition that the said William should build on the said piece of land an hospital house for the poor for ever whose entry should be without gift of gold, silver or paying any salary or profit to anyone, called the Town's Almhouse to hold 4 of the most poor and impotent persons of the town'. This building remained until 1836 when it was moved to Vineyard Road.

The increasing extension of the use of the land to the east of the town, and the occupations of the owners, can be seen from the following documents of 1590. They show that the commonalty were working with the burgesses in allocating the land which was becoming available for farming.

'The Commonalty of Newport with assent of all the Burgesses to Thomas Peate of Newport, tanner, A piece of wasteland lying in the hoiles towards Norbroom to build upon . . . '

To Thomas Hawkins, mercer, 'Land in the Warden's Crofts'.

To William Whitmore of Newport, 'A piece of land with a barn built on it in the Hoyles in or next to a field called Norbrome near a way leading from a lane called the Bakehouse Lane to a house of Thomas Peyte called a tannehouse'. Bakehouse Lane became Stafford Street with the tanhouse at the bottom.

The agriculture of the surrounding area was in a prosperous state. Wool and woollen products were playing an important part in the economy of the nation as well as locally. The local breed of sheep was crossed with Cannock Chase rams to develop a strong sheep with a long staple, suitable for the cloth of that day. This was a well-grown sheep, clipping about seven to 10 lbs. of strong wool, a factor which meant the wool fetched a high price.

In terms of today, however, Newport was still a very small town or large village. Individuals, however, like Robert Cathyn, gentleman and John Marshall, citizen and cloth worker of London, could own substantial estates. They each had a moiety of each of the manors of Edgmond and Newport: '100 messuages, 40 acres of crops, 40 cottages, 2 water mills, 500 acres of land, 100 acres meadow, 500 acres pasture, 500 acres of wood, 1,000 acres of furze and heath, 100 acres of water, 10s. of rent with common pasture for 500 sheep and 100 animals'.

Out of 18 livestock markets in Shropshire, seven were specialising in cattle — Oswestry, Shrewsbury, Wellington, Ludlow, Whitchurch, Bridgnorth and Newport. A 1670 report on the market shows the importance it had achieved, by the kinds of stock sold, and the distance the buyers and sellers travelled to reach it.

> Newport.   The Tolls Recorded at the ffaire there holden the fifteenth day of September in the tenth year of the Reigne of our most gratious Sovereigne Lorde Charles by the Grace of God King of England, Scotland, ffrance and Ireland, Defender of the Fathe etc, before Thomas Tomkyns great Steward there.
>
> Joane Twiner of Eaton upon Tearne in the parish of Stoke Com Salop sould one black bullock price 1li. 13s. 8d.
>
> Thomas Derrington of Ammington Com Staff. sould unto Richard Adeney of Uppington Com Staff. one browne bullock price 4li. 5s. 10d.
>
> Thomas Dodd, Wellington sould two bullocks, one browne the other black, price 12li. 5s. 0d.
>
> Thomas Shutser of Chessidyne hath solde six sheeps to Richard Fennyhouse of Wheaton Aston in Salop price 10li. 20d.
>
> John Inglethroppe of lyleshull hath solde a bull black aged 2 years to the servants of John Fowkes of Gunston 3li. 6s. 8d.
>
> George Jackson of Pyllington Hall hath solde two oxen black to John Offley of Newport 10li. 6s. 8d.
>
> Thomas Spendlove Walton on Chubb, Staffs. sould one black cowe with eare part white with a calfe price 3li. 11s.
>
> Thomas Raynold has solde six swynne whereof one is a boare and whereof 4 are white and the other two are spotted and the price are 14s. apiece abating 2s. for one of them.

A busy High Street with the womenfolk getting the week's shopping while the quiet men were moving among the cattle noticing the eyes and horns to tell them what they wanted to know; the squareness of the beef bullocks and the sleekness of the milk cows, pinching the flanks; hands under the belly to find the milk vein, fingers for the milk well; choosing a cow for the wife to milk for the house. 'Meeting you like a princess, leaving you like a dairymaid' as they used to say.

An entry in the Parish Register tells us 'that upon Saturday, ye 28 november 1663 was first horse Market begun that ever was in this Towne of Newport'. An excerpt from the market record gives us the flavour of this special market:

> Thomas Shelton of Sleape Com Salop sould one gray mare 4 years ould trotting to William Skett of Heathfield Com Staffs price pledge Thomas Mountford of Sleape pd. 2li. 14s. 4d.
>
> James Baker of the Lea in the parish of High Offley in the County of Staff. sould one black nagg ambling to Thomas Bradley of Donnington Com Salop price 2li. 16s. 4d.
>
> Wm Sherratt of Leigh Com Staff. sould one Chestnut bay mare trotting with a ship on the nose and a Starre price 3li. 19s.
>
> Edward Collier parish of Bishops Offley sould one great ambling mare trotter with Thomas Breadeley of Donnington for a sorrel nagge ambler upon open hand touch.

This was most probably held in what is now the Victoria Park area. One can imagine the sly looks; the hands on the withers looking for galls; down to the fetlocks for spavins; the ribald shouts as the horse was trotted; the keen look to see how the handler turned the nag; and the final spit on the palms of the hand before they struck together to seal the bargain.

Newport, on the road to Chester, which was then the port to connect with Ireland, was constantly in touch with London as travellers stopped on their way to and from the port. But Newport was not only an overnight stop for travellers, but a supply depot for the surrounding agricultural area where changes were much slower in coming into operation. Looking at farming methods today the change brought about by mechanisation makes it almost impossible to visualise the former life and attitudes of the rural community. To realise that so many changes have taken place within living memory is even more difficult. I sometimes think I was fortunate to get a glimpse of the past by being tutored by the last generation of traditionally-minded farm workers in the 1920s. This was a life where the waggoners 'baited' their horses at 5 o'clock in the morning ready for yoking out at 7 o'clock; where the gang of handmilkers worked between first and second breakfasts, so that one of the daughters could get two small churns on a yoke across her shoulders and go around the village ladling out the supply, while her elder brother slung the twelve-gallon churns onto a trap to deliver it farther afield. I remember turning an end-over-end butter churn and waiting for that magic swish-swish that would not come because of the thunder in the air; clipping sheep with shears, castrating lambs with my teeth because I had 'the best set of teeth in the gang'; 30 people in a hay field ricking the hay; cutting the corn and tying sheaves by hand with the straw instead of string; stooking, loading wagons, building and thatching stacks; carrying 18 stone of seed wheat on my shoulders because 'I was 16 years old'; killing and curing a pig.

19. Churning butter.

The first contact that Newport had with the upheaval caused by the Civil War was in September 1642 when Charles I, with his 12-year-old son, passed through Newport and Donnington on his way to review his troops at Wellington. Prince Rupert, at the same time, was moving eight troops of dragoons from Stafford to take Bridgnorth. The first contact of note with the Parliamentary forces came in February 1643 when Lord Brooke reached Lichfield with 15,000 dragoons. His advance guard is said to have reached Newport.

In September of that year Colonel Thomas Mytton of Halston was recruiting in Market Drayton prior to capturing Wem. Following this, Sir William Brereton occupied Longford House, the property of the earl of Shrewsbury. On 28 December Tong castle fell to the Parliamentary forces. On 25 March 1644 Colonel Mytton led an attack on Lilleshall Abbey, which was fortified by Sir Richard Leveson for the Royalists, who sent for reinforcements from Wellington. After some manoeuvring, the battle was joined at Longford and Mytton's troops were routed with the loss of 200 men. When the canal was being constructed through Newport a grave containing several skeletons, apparently of Cromwellian soldiers, was unearthed. A recent find of cannon balls in Brookside Avenue and Hallcroft Gardens would suggest that the battle was fought all along the Strine Valley. A month later Longford surrendered to the Royalist Sergeant Major Skrimshaw. He allowed Captain Parry and 100 musketeers to march away without weapons with 'their hands in their pockets'.

Although Shrewsbury had fallen to Parliament in March 1645, King Charles passed through Newport on 7 May, staying at Chetwynd with Mr. Thomas Pigott, who had served as a Captain in the dragoons for two months at the beginning of the war. Captain Stone, hearing that a party of Royalists was quartered in Newport, led a Parliamentary force from Stafford on 20 May 'killing a captain and 20 soldiers and bringing away 60 horse'. In August, Lilleshall Abbey surrendered to the Parliamentarians.

In May 1646 Charles I surrendered to the Scottish Army who handed him over to the English Parliament, and he was subsequently executed in 1649. His son Charles landed in Scotland in 1650, proclaimed himself King, and with a Scottish army, marched into England where they were defeated at Worcester (1651). The King with 60 gentlemen for bodyguard escaped northwards, arriving at Boscobel, where the King took off his insignia, giving his diamond badge of the Garter ('George') to a Colonel Blague. Leaving the King safe at Boscobel the Duke of Buckingham, Earl of Derby, Earl of Lauderdale, Lord Talbot, Lord Wilmot and Colonel Blague marched north to Newport which they had learnt was held by Cromwell's men. In the ensuing skirmish Lord Talbot escaped to Longford Hall, where he hid for some time before escaping to the Continent.

The Duke of Buckingham and the others turned aside on to an old road through Field Aston to Forton. They then took the road now called Shray Lane to Langot Valley where they were attacked by Colonel Lilburne's men from the front and in the rear by Colonel Blundel

20. A Civil War foot-soldier.

in charge of the pursuit. The Duke of Buckingham and Colonel Blague managed to escape through the fields and were befriended by a local farmer in Bloore Park, near

Cheswardine, in whose house Colonel Blague hid the 'George'. The Colonel was captured but the 'George' later found its way into the hands of Mr. Izaak Walton, who returned it to Colonel Blague in the Tower of London. The Duke of Buckingham managed to hide in a nearby cave, and after many adventures joined the King who had escaped to France.

Every parish was obliged to muster a 'trained band' of local men to protect their homes or to form part of a national army, but in the Civil War, with no definite boundaries and fighting their own countrymen, there were many deserters who fled back to their homes or, indeed, changed sides. It was hard for ordinary people to understand why they should keep paying out to both sides. Newport was ostensibly Royalist in sympathy; nevertheless, when the King's assessment of contributions for the army was due, the collectors who came to Newport were refused payment and 'had hands laid on them'.

The only monument to the Civil War in Newport is the plinth of the Puleston Cross, erected in memory of Sir Roger de Puleston, a local knight who was killed fighting the Welsh. This was decapitated by the Parliamentarians, and there are also the cannon balls which have been found in the Church Aston side of the town.

One of the most notable events in the history of the town is thus described in the parish register.

> On the ffridaye in the afternoone beeinge the 19th daye of May Anno 1665 a sudden furyous fire arose whiche began in the house of Richd. Shotton, a smith, living at the Chiltop, whiche by Saturdaye noone followinge were burned out of habitation about 162 familyes besides the better of 10 more of houses puld to pieces — and much prevented. Newport sin no more, lest a worse punyshment b'fall thee. The losse to Newport was 30,000 pounds.
>
> T. MILLINGTON

In order to help in the rebuilding and rehabilitation of the town, Charles II issued a plea for aid for the distressed.

> Charles the Second by the Grace of God, King of England, Scotland, France and Ireland, Defender of the Faith etc. Whereas upon the 19th day of May in the 17th year of our reign between the hours of 3 and 4 o'clock in the afternoon a most sudden, fearful and dismal fire happened in our market town of Newport in our County of Salop, which within the space of a few hours consumed and burnt to ashes above one hundred and fifty and six inhabitations, so that the whole loss sustained by the said fire doth amount in all to the sum of £23,948 and upwards to the ruin of most of the inhabitants of the said town, their wives and children, unless they be speedily supported and relieved by the Charitable Benevolence of well-disposed Christians. We do hereby recommend their sufferings to the charity of our loving subjects, that in this case their Bowels of Compassion will be the more enlarged, and their charity extended to those distressed inhabitants who at mid-day full and flourishing in good buildings, ample furniture, plentiful provisions and store of necessities and before midnight deprived of all, made empty and nothing, compelled to lodge in open air, and seek hospitality at the hand of others. Give a portion to seven, and also to eight for thou knowest not what evil may be upon the Earth.
>
> In witness of this we have caused these our letters to be made Patent for the space of six whole years next after the date hereof to endure no longer. Witness ourselves at Westminster the fifteenth day of October in the eighteenth year of our reign.
>
> God Save the King

The church and the grammar school escaped the fire, as did the Guildhall (1615) and the black and white Smallwood Lodge.

In 1632 William Barnfield had built a house 'to sell butter and cheese in' near Puleston Cross. This must have been a wooden structure as it was destroyed in the fire in May. This building, known as the Butter Cross, 'being destroyed when the town was burnt, was rebuilt by the Hon. Thos Talbot Esq. of Longford and was reared the 24th day of November 1665'. The new building was of stone.

In 1547 a description was given of 'waste between the Booth Hall and a tenement in length from the street called Swynne Crosse to an empty parcel of land adjoining the almhouse'. Swynne Crosse must have been the forerunner of New Street, for when that street was constructed a trough was destroyed which had been used for feeding the pigs in the pig market. At the corner of New Street is a building dated 1667, which was rebuilt after the fire as the *Britannia Inn*.

As the burgesses' Book of Orders and Elections had been destroyed in the fire, it was decided to ask counsel's opinion on various questions, one of which was 'who must put and keep the streets in repair since burgesses' rents are so sunk that it is impossible that they can do it?'. Counsel's answer was: 'if there is no particular custom or bye-law for repairing, I conceive they must be repaired as in other towns. Of common right, the parish ought to repair the streets as part of the highways within the parish and it will be incumbent on the parish to lay the burden of the repair on some other prescriptions. And if lands, dedicated to bear the costs are concealed, or have been conveyed away so as they cannot now be fixed to be subject to this charge, the former charge on the parish will survive'. Counsel added further that: 'I am led to conclude that the burgesses are a corporate body, having a perpetual succession, and in that view originally, it is reasonable to suppose that the inhabitants were made into that body'. This meant that as a corporate body the town was responsible for

---

ENTRY OF A BURGESS

The Date is the Day of General Meeting when such Burgesses are Chose and Entered in the Burgesses Book which is signed by the High Steward, Bayliffs and other Burgesses there present or the Major part of them if not unanimous where any Dissent is.

Know all men by those presents that We the Burgesses of New Borough otherwise Newport in the County of Salop with one assent and consent   Receive and Admitt   William Adams of the Wood in the Parish of Child's Ercall in the said County of Salop Esquire into the Number of Burgesses of the Vill and Borough of New Borough.   And that the said William Adams shall have and from henceforth Enjoy for him and his heirs such Liberties, Privilegies and Advantages as anyone or other the Burgesses.   In Testimony whereof we have hereinto putt our Common Seal Dated at Newport the Eight day of June in the Twenty Sixth year of the Reign of our Sovereign Lord George the second by the grace of God of Great Britain France and Ireland. King, Defender of the faith and so forth.   [1753].

the bridge, since in 1531 it had been decreed that the county was responsible for bridges except in corporate towns. A memo in the records says 'The books burnt in the fire has deprived us of the names of the former High Stewards but by Deed without Date John de Weston of Weston under Elizabeth, and by another paper Sir Francis Newport was in the reign of Charles I before High Steward of the Borough of Newport'.

An interesting question arose at this time as to whether or not a younger son could succeed his father as a burgess on the death of the eldest son. This was brought up by a William Richardson whose father and grandfather had been burgesses before 1668. Counsel's findings were that the original charter was to the burgesses and their heirs. Therefore no younger son could be a burgess while the heir or his heir was alive. 'It might be inconvenient if the Law should revive such an antiquated right, and it may be one reason why a younger brother should not inherit.' It was also stated that 'no woman [was] to be a Burgess'.

The lords of the manor disputed the right of 'Foreigners' to be elected to the burgess roll claiming that 'by the book in being it appears the Neighbouring Gentlemen and others, Farmers, have been chosen and neverafter paid toll'. Counsel's opinion was that 'usage may warrant foreigners to be admitted to that body'. It would seem that quite a few of the burgesses did not reside in the town.

As the fire was reputed to have destroyed the records of the burgesses we find diffi-culty in estimating the growth of the town during the first 300 years of its existence. However, there are several documents extant which we can take into consideration.

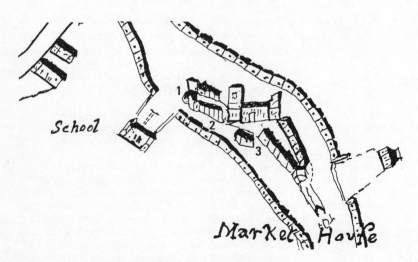

21. Central Newport, from Hill's map, 1680.

In 1680 William Hill was contracted to map the land of Church Aston but not that of Newport. He did, however, map the High Street (without burgage strips) and the pool. The limit of the pool on the map is about the site of the present Summerhouse Bridge, about half the original stretch of water. This we can assume was the result of the towns-people having drained the top end to convert it to agricultural use. Looking at the map, we notice two outruns at the dam. In early indentures only one mill was mentioned in the Edgmond and Newport manors, but a later one lists 'two water mills'. We find later, that the canal removed the mill on the north side of the present bridge. There was, however, the remains of a mill race at Vauxhall which was fed by the south run (shown on the map). Thus the town, by lowering the level of the dam, gained the land and regulated the overflow for an extra mill. The map of the High Street shows it built up from Wellington Road to the bridge so that the damage created by the fire must have been repaired in the succeeding 15 years.

A note on religion

Between A.D. 656 and 669 the spiritual care of the district of Newport was in the hands of the bishops of Mercia. In 669 the See of Lichfield was founded by the Arch-bishop of Canterbury with St Chad as the patron saint of the diocese. We have already seen that there was a religious community here, or monks in residence, in 963. Later Newport came under the Coventry diocese.

The first mention of a priest in Newport is that of Richard 'Priest of Newport', who witnessed the charter granted by Henry I. In 1129 the church, an aisle-less nave and chancel, was confirmed to the Abbey of St Peter and Paul, Shrewsbury by Bishop Clinton. This situation remained until 1452 when Thomas Draper purchased the church and established a Chantry. The last recorded priest in charge of the area under the jurisdiction of the Pope was Roger Salter of Salter Hall.

When any form of worship is accepted as the national religion then those who do not subscribe to it can become, in the eyes of the state, enemies of the government. An old statute of *praemunire* was sometimes quoted, 'a writ charging with the offence of resorting to a foreign jurisdiction'. This was used against the Catholics by Henry VIII, identifying the Pope as the foreign power. Those who clung to the 'old faith' found that the obligation on all citizens to attend church services regularly was against their conscience. It was the constables' duty to report to the vestry those who consistently refused to attend, and they would be fined. Between 1592 and 1683 there were 79 instances of persons in Edgmond, Newport, Chetwynd, Longford and Church Aston arraigned for this offence. These included Thomas Talbot, Esq., owner of the manors of Longford and Church Aston, the wife of Robert Pigott, Justice of the Peace, and various lesser persons down to Joseph Challinor, labourer. The fines ranged from 'half of his lands', to sixty pounds. Thomas Talbot was named in the 'act for Disarming Papists' (1680) as refusing to take the oath of Allegiance.

The religious census of the inhabitants over the age of 16 years in Newport Deanery in 1676 makes interesting reading.

	Con-formists	Papists	Non-Com	Total	PERCENTAGE		
					Papists	Non-Com	Total Non-Com
Albrighton	267	23	1	291	8%	½%	8½%
Edgmond	607	17	9	633	3%	1½%	4½%
Longford	77	6	1	85	9%	1½%	10½%
Newport	706	9	30	745	1%	4%	5%

Were the Papists in Albrighton, Edgmond and Longford, country people who loyally clung to the 'old faith' or were they paying lip-service to the Catholic landowners for whom they worked? Did the Anglicans in Newport ensure a continuance of the stability of the town or were the five per cent. of Nonconformists the yeast which provided the boost to the development which kept Newport the main town in the area?

Dissenters continued to flourish in the Newport area in the late 17th century and later. We read in the Parish Church Register of 1662 that the vicar, 'Honest Mr. Malden' had been 'forced from his Ministry for Nonconformity this month'. Mr. Malden continued to live in Newport and preach in the neighbourhood, joining with others to form an Independent Church. He died in 1681. A note in the parish register on his death reads 'so much learning, piety, and humility, I have not seen this great while layd in a grave; but blessed be God we had such a one so long'.

Mr. John Jones, a native of Newport, was expelled from Oxford University in 1765 with five other students. It was claimed that they 'had offered up extempore prayers, preached at Conventicles, connected themselves with Methodists, expounded the Scriptures, not being in Holy Orders, and that they held the doctrine of election and that the working of God's Spirit was irresistible'. Mr. Jones later settled in the town, preaching and holding meetings.

22. Candle and pewter plates.

V

NOVA PORTA

This name is still used by the grammar school. The word 'port' has been misconstrued by some people to suggest that Newport had been a seaport. 'Port' was the medieval word meaning the area covered by the market charter.

Speaking of traffic on the roads in the 17th century T. S. Willan says 'It is possible that there was a considerable movement of goods between London and Cheshire, for it formed part of the great London and Holyhead Road'. As Newport was on this road the traffic between the two was of prime importance to the town. The price for the carriage of goods into the town was a matter of concern. It had come to the notice of the government that 'diverse Waggoners and other Carriers by combination among themselves have raised the prices of the carriage of goods'. In an Act of 1692 the Justices of the Peace were required 'to assess and rate the prices of Land Carriage Goods brought within their jurisdiction by any Waggoner or Carrier'. The rates set by Shropshire were 5s. per hundredweight from 1 May to 1 November and 6s. per hundredweight in the winter months. The rate set for Cheshire was 5s. per hundredweight and 7s. per hundredweight respectively. The rate for pack horses was 1d. per pound.

By the 17th century the chapman on his horse had been superseded by caravans of horses carrying much heavier loads. One of the earliest carriers, Pickford, started his haulage business in 1649 with pack horses carrying 100 lb. of goods in panniers over long distances. The next development was the horse- or ox-drawn wagon capable of carrying the equivalent load of five pack horses and bulky articles unsuitable for panniers. The amount of stabling and feeding required from a stopping place like Newport was considerable.

Today we find it hard to realise the difficulties of movement between settlements. Transporting goods was the main problem as trade increased. With the increase in long distance travel it became obvious that, for various reasons, the main roads in some parishes fell far short of what was necessary to carry the traffic adequately. In 1531 it had been decreed that the county was responsible for bridges outside the towns, but all householders and labourers in a parish had to give eight hours in four days of the year for the upkeep of roads and, in Easter Week, the constables and church wardens had to elect two persons to be surveyors for all roads and bridges in their parish.

23. A wandering vagrant.

In the country, where the highways had had the trees cut back since early times, the chapmen with their string of pack horses could always find a path, but the heavy transport wagons had hard work, especially in winter, to find a suitable route. In the towns like Newport the effect of the concentration of all this traffic on one street can be imagined.

As well as the coaches and wagons, there were the post chaises. These were small closed chariots with limited luggage, travelling at a gallop. The posting houses hired these carriages to travellers for ninepence to one shilling per mile, complete with post boys. The inns would hire a change of horses to pull one's own carriage or hire a change of horses for the post chaises, or single riding. Travellers purchased a day ticket and mileage ticket, and left them with the toll keeper at the first turnpike gate. These were returned to the Stamp Office at the *Old Red Lion*, St Mary Street where the tax or annual licence — five shillings plus a halfpenny per travelling mile — was recovered from the posting inn.

The mail was first carried by horseback in 1720, but as this became unprofitable on account of losses by theft, a mail coach carrying a shotgun guard was instituted. The first trial run was from Bristol to London in 1784 and by 1791 one was running from London to Shrewsbury with cross-country deliveries at certain points. A horse post left Newport every morning at six to meet the London to Holyhead mails at Shifnal, and returned every evening with the London and northern letters at half past five, 'going on to meet the Manchester Mail'.

The increasing cost of road repair, and the obvious inability (and unwillingness) of many parishes to carry it out satisfactorily, led to the introduction of 'turnpike' roads. Groups of local gentlemen joined together to pay for a stretch of road to be thoroughly repaired; they then put a gate or 'turnpike' across each end and charged tolls on vehicles wishing to use it.

In 1760 the road from Chester to Newport through Whitchurch and on to Ivetsy Bank and Castle Bromwich was turnpiked. In 1778 a further Act allowed 'making a Road of communication to the present turnpike Road from Newport to Eccleshall'.

The improved roads and better standards of coach building made journeys easier both in terms of time and comfort. A coach was expected to travel about fifty miles a day, with changes of horses. Any innkeeper who wished to take a share in the coaching trade provided horses for his 'ground' or stint. The wide alleyways between the shops in Newport High Street are the remains of the entrances to the inn yards. These were built-over as part of the inn with the opening high enough to let the coach through. The passengers paying for the dearer seats inside the coach took their places in the inn yard while the outside passengers had to climb up in the street. By 1789 Barfoot and Wilkes were listing 'a coach from

24. Milestone situated near Post Office on Lower Bar.

The Red Lion, Newport to London Tuesday, Thursday and Saturday morning, at four o'clock; and one for Chester the same evenings at eleven o'clock'. Goods went to London every Tuesday morning at four o'clock by Scott's wagon and by Cheswell's cart to Wellington and Shifnal on Tuesdays.

Surviving records show us changes in land use around the town. In 1750 Thomas Parsons, carpenter, took some 'waste land called the Flags, late of the Lords of the Manor of Newport called the Poole, formerly covered with water and the Newport Mill Pool at the lower end'. Nearer the town a doctor had a field, probably for grazing the horses he would need on his country calls: 'To William Miller, Surgeon and Apothecary, the close of land . . . at a place called the Holes on one side of the brook called the Strine and at the upper end the Caldercrofts, adjoining the Vineyard'.

Some of the land was being used for commercial rather than agricultural purposes. 'To John Peate, Saddler . . . a little close of land with the lime pits near the Flaggs'. This would have been for use in connection with the tannery. William Hurd, 'General Dealer', had 'three closes of land called the Water Pieces at the top end of Vineyard Road and the Strine Brook for reservation of timber and minerals'. The minerals referred to were a sand pit which survived into this century.

Several street names appear about this time. In 1792 Bakehouse Lane (a changed name from Stafford Street); in 1738 Beaumaris Lane; in 1788 Mason's Place; in 1766 Gravel Walk or Stepping Stones; and in 1740 Water Lane.

There are several references to 'hemp butts'. These were pieces of land used for growing flax and hemp. The fibres of the plants were worked out after harvesting to be used for cloth and cords. In the days of the long bows in the 16th century a bonus was paid for hemp fibres for the bowstrings.

Building development was also taking place up to the county boundary. The types of houses are suggested by the two examples from 1741:

> To John Jervis, Yeoman. A tenement or burgage lately erected on Burgesses' land, containing four little rooms and 3 chambers, with the pig sty and house of office adjoining in the Hoyles fronting to a way at the bottom of Backhouse Lane, leading to the Hoyles and lying backward up to a little brook running at the bottom of the yard and to void or waste grounds near the tan yard.

> To Christina Parsons, Spinster. The tenement formerly erected on the burgesses' land containing 3 little rooms and 3 chambers over the same with the garden hemp butt and void ground shooting up to the buildings of John Hodgkiss, butcher, fronting to the lane at the bottom of the Backhouse Lane, leading to the Great Marsh, and lying backwards to the little brook running at the bottom of Harvery's Yard (possibly the Strine); and the other garden to a stable of John Hodgkiss and waste ground near the washing pit lately in the possession of William Parsons, Stonemason.

This could perhaps be what is now known as Parson's Barn. The Strine was still flowing past the Water Pieces or Caldercroft, but the land had some use for occupation although, with the peat deposits, wet weather would make residence only seasonal.

The successful merchants and manufacturers were buying estates, amalgamating smaller farms and enclosing available land. A report in the Sutherland estate papers explains the reasons:

> The arrangement which was adopted for the improvement of this property was, laying the lands together, in farms of considerable extent, varying in size according to the nature of the soil, and other circumstances, and in this respect, following the same course as had been adopted in arranging the coast side farms in Sutherland, being the constant, invariable, and necessary progress of society in this respect.

The enclosure of land to form a few large estates often meant a loss of independence for smallholders, who became tenants of the estate owners. The Reverend Henry Plymley, an ardent supporter of enclosure, wrote:

> Let those who doubt, go round the commons now open and view the poor, ill-cultivated, impoverished spots erected for which they paid 6d. of 1s. a year which afforded them a very trifle towards maintenance and yet operates on their minds as a sort of independence.
> This idea leads the man to lose many days work by which he gets a habit of indolence. The surrounding farmers by this means have neither industrious labourers nor servants, and the contrary is the case where they live under the farmer, in comfortable cottages with only a quarter of an acre of land, work every day of the year and have their children taught to read and put out to labour early.

He concluded his argument by saying that the daughters, not having enough to do, were tempted to a reputedly more profitable occupation.

A further reorganisation of the use of the land, and also of the conduct of the affairs of the town came in May 1750. An indenture between the Earl of Shrewsbury and Earl Gower, lords of the manor of Newport, and Robert Pigott of Chetwynd, the Steward of the borough of Newport, and the burgesses granted 'Thomas Parsons and his heirs, all these pieces of land called Newport Pool and Pool Place, and also that parcel of and adjoining thereto called the Flaggs. In trust that the Stone Bridge or Pool Dam should in the first place be repaired and as to the surplus of the said rents and profits In Trust they should be applied to keeping in good order, the pavement of the street, or in repairing the Market House or Town Hall at the discretion of the Trustees. The above premises were conveyed by Thomas Parsons to the Trustees thus inaugurating the Bridge Trust'.

The trustees offered a petition in 1763:

> A large parcel of waste land called the Great Marsh is become of little advantage to the said Burgesses as by draining and improving the said Marsh and increasing the same, the profits of the said Marsh will be thoroughly advantaged to all, and the Burgesses will be enabled to pave the streets (in better manner than heretofore) which are broad and extensive and lie in the Great Road between Chester and London with heavy carriages from the coal pits and if unsufficient then the charge for repairing the streets must fall on the parish.

This land had been given as Common pasture by Nicholas de Audley in 1292. The representation by the burgesses resulted in an Act of Parliament of George III in 1764.

The Newport Salop Marsh Improvement Act

> Whereas there is within the township of Newport, in the county Salop, a common waste ground called the Marsh, containing one hundred and seventeen acres or thereabouts, wherein each household in the said town has from time immemorial had a right of turning, which privilege has proved of very little advantage of the said town but rather an inconvenience by increasing the poor thereof. And whereas the Right Honourable George Earl of Shrewsbury, and the Right Honourable Granville, Earl of Gower are lords of the manor of Newport aforesaid. And whereas the Earl of Shrewsbury is entitled to four beast gates in the said Marsh, and whereas the said Marsh is wet and Boggy and cannot in its present situation be cultivated to any considerable advantage, but is capable of being improved. And whereas it is apprehended, that the enclosing and improving the said Marsh, and applying the profits thereof from time to time, after making satisfaction to the Lords of the Manor for their respective rights therein, in paving and keeping in repair the streets of the said town of Newport, and in repairing and keeping in repair the Market Hall and Cross there and also in establishing and encouraging some manufacture in the said town and apprenticing the children of the poor parishioners of Newport aforesaid, would be of very great advantage to the said town in general, and may be a means of extending the manufactory throughout the neighbourhood.

A survey found the marsh to be 111 acres, three rods and 31 poles, of which four acres were allotted to the earl in lieu of his four beast gates. The remainder of the marsh was to be subject to the payment of 20s. chief rent.

Eventually, however, the marsh trustees bought the four acres from the earl. This was in fact the first enclosure of common owned land, and resulted in the formation of the Marsh Trustees, a body separate from the burgesses, who controlled the business of the town. But the decision did not meet with universal acclaim. Four men took their beasts down and turned them into the Marsh. They were apprehended by the police of the day and locked in the market hall. One of them objected to this: this led to 'The Riot of Newport'.

In 1790 the Marsh Trustees established 'a manufactory to employ poor children in fabricating stockings and other woollen merchandise'. This was good employment for the children but, as it was run at a loss, it had to be closed down.

The price of grinding corn was causing some concern and a windmill was erected at a cost of £2,000. This too was a financial loss and it was sold in 1802 for £1,000.

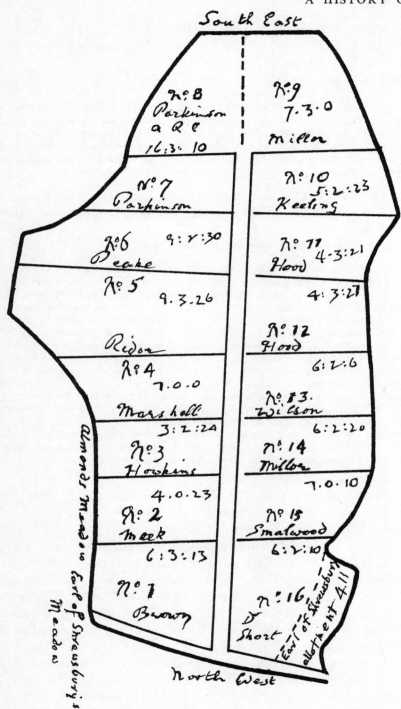

25. Division of the enclosed marsh, 1767.

It was used as a dwelling at one time until it was demolished and the ground used for houses.

COURT PROCEEDINGS FOLLOWING THE RIOT CAUSED BY THE ENCLOSURE OF THE MARSH

The King against William Allin

Upon an Indictment for Private Breaking at Newport in the County of Salop

On the 11th June Last George Appleby was for riotous assembling himself with severall others confined by the said Constables in the Town Hall and locked therein in Order to take him before a Justice. But the Prisoner with John Holding forced their way to the Door of the said Town Hall. And the Prisoner with an Axe Broak and Shattered the said Door in two parts and rescued the said Prisoner George Appleby. And with the Axe in his hand in a riotus manner and in Company with several rioters walked about the Streets of Newport.

---

26. Public Notice concerning Riotous Assembly.

The geology of the underlying strata of the neighbouring area once again played a part in the development of the town. An outcrop of limestone in Church Aston and Lilleshall led to extensive mining operations during the later 18th and early 19th centuries. A very comprehensive and detailed account has been published by D. R. Adams and J. Hazeley in the *Records of the Shropshire Mining Club*, which has been much drawn on for what follows.

Lime can be used as a flux in iron smelting, in agricultural practices and probably the first open cast mining in Lilleshall (17th century) was for building requirements. The limestone was broken up, mixed with coal, and slow-burned in a kiln to make a white powder which, slaked and mixed with sand, made a mortar to bind the building bricks together. The discovery by Abraham Darby of how to make coke from coal led to an increase in iron smelting and the need for a good supply of suitable lime.

An increase in iron production in the Coalbrookdale area called for a greater output in the supply of lime. As Lilleshall lime was of the best quality, a busy mining and lime making industry developed in Church Aston and Lilleshall. When the open cast workers went deeper they ran into one of the difficulties met by miners — a geological fault. This is a crack in the earth's surface, caused in this instance by the volcanic activity which resulted in Lilleshall Hill, which meant that pits had to be sunk to meet the increased demand, as one ton of lime was needed to produce one ton of pig iron. As the mines went deeper, a different limestone was discovered which was found to have the property of setting under water. This led to a very busy trade with the harbour builders in the development of Liverpool, the limestone being transported through Newport.

The pits at Church Aston and Lilleshall both encountered disastrous flooding in 1860 which they were unable to overcome and, although the Wildmore pits carried on for another 20 years, 100 years of a busy industry supplying 26,000 tons of lime a year came to an end. Lilleshall reverted to a village, but dwellings still there and at Church Aston are the result of the busy limestone mines. Newport too had had its share in the trade while it lasted.

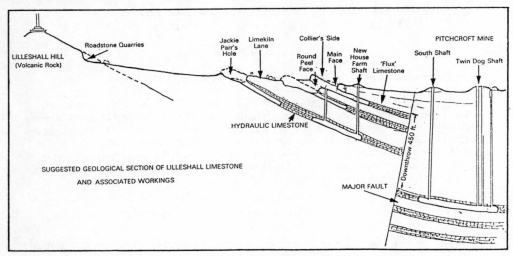

26. This is part of the east-west fault which skirts Newport.
(By David Roye Adams).

At a meeting of the Inhabitants of the Parish of Newport,
in the presence of the following. Notice 23rd August 1832.

The inhabitants of the Town of Newport are requested to meet up in the Vestry at 11 o'clock on Thursday next to consider whether and what steps should be taken to procure the appointment of a board of health to name suitable persons for members of the same and to consult as to any other measures which may be proposed as precautions for the approach of Cholera or as expedient to be adopted in case the parish should be unhappily visited by it.

Ordered: that the Rev. W. Sandford do take the Chair.

Ordered: that a Board of Health be established at Newport and that the following Gentlemen be appointed members of the same: Wm. Woodall, J. B. Baddeley, Esq., R. Higgins, Esq., G. H. Duncalf, Esq., James Lindof, Esq., C. Morris, Esq., Rev. W. Sandford, Rev. E. Meredith, J. Stanley, Esq.

The need for help in sickness led to friendly societies which lasted well into this century being formed for the benefit of the working classes. A society was formed in Newport in 1779 with 208 members, 'for the relief of such members as may by sickness or any other infirmity be incapable of following their respective employments, also to encourage industry, and improve every other Social Virtue that inspires to the Good of Mankind in general, and this Society in particular'. The prospectus went on to state that

A few years past it might have been necessary to have selected a few arguments arising from the establishment of Societies of this nature, especially to the lower classes of mankind, but the benefits are now so well known and daily experienced, that none but a hoodwinked reasoner would ever attempt to prove them useless or detrimental to any Individual. From the contribution of six pence each Member in case of Death, which more than defrays the expense of a funeral. The Society's Annual subscription of Two Guineas to the Salop Infirmary is an extraordinary advantage to us, we have thereby right to recommend two in-patients within the year, and I believe as many out-patients are entitled to assistance of an experienced surgeon at home. Otherwise he goes to the Infirmary and all possible care is taken of him. He pays nothing for his maintenance, and at the same time has the comfortable reflection that his family receives five shillings per week.

Those who could not afford the help of a friendly society were dependent on the parish welfare arrangements. A Poor Law Act of 1722 allowed parishes to form unions with a board of guardians to administer their affairs. Meeting every fortnight, the guardians of the Newport Union had the following parishes in their jurisdiction: Adbaston (Stafford), Cherrington, Chetwynd, Chetwynd Aston, Edgmond, Forton (Stafford), Gnosall (Stafford), High Offley (Stafford), Lilleshall, Longford, Newport, Norbury (Stafford), Tibberton, Weston Jones (Stafford), and Woodcote. The Union covered the area from which persons could go to and from the centre of administration in a single day. A poorhouse was built on Vineyard Road.

Trade and industry

Town directories, like the Domesday Book, are not guaranteed to give a full picture of a town but we can get a good picture of the occupations of the inhabitants and, over the years, shifts in the services offered to the town. In Barfoot and Wilkes' directory of 1789 we find many trades and services listed. Five tailors are listed and three specialist breeches makers. Today jeans and denim overalls are the universal wear for tractor drivers, but walking in an eight-inch furrow behind a pair of horses, calls for different attire around the lower legs, especially on wet clayey lands. As most transport was by horseback, breeches were the natural choice for riders. The fashion for the labourers changed later of course, to the moleskins of the canal navvies with a strap under their knees to give freedom of movement. Headgear was catered for by two hatters, three straw hat makers and — obviously one for the gentry — a peruke or wig maker.

We get the impression that a good deal of home dressmaking was the norm for the ladies, for only three milliners are listed, but there were ample supplies of material from three mercers, two drapers and two dyers. Three stay-makers were employed in the town — a profession carried on well into this century by ladies who visited their clients to get the necessary measurements. The modern foundation garments have made these ladies redundant, the last one in Newport ceasing business in 1980. For the more exotic dresses, there was one mantua maker. Four hairdressers had establishments in the town.

Not all the retailers had premises, however, three hucksters (18th century barrow boys) being listed.

As would be expected, the majority of the services were in food and clothing. An interesting omission, in view of the town's connection with fish, is the mention

27. Huckster's stall.

of any fish retailers, although eight butchers are mentioned. It is very much later before we find fish merchants mentioned among the town retailers.

Leather working was the main industry, with skinners, curriers and leather cutters. The tannery, situated at what is now called Tan Bank, was in operation before the 17th century, next to a stream which flowed into the River Strine. This stream divided the town from the Vineyard area. The Marsh Brook was later piped across the playing fields and under the canal into the Strine. Boots and shoes were made by hand, occupying eight shoemakers. The harness work for the horses was taken care of by three saddlers.

There was a timber yard in the town to supply the needs of the various workers in wood. This was of course, a necessity in house construction and repairs. It would seem that four plumbers and glaziers were too many in proportion to the population. There was one plasterer, and one mason who also supplied gravestones.

A good many of the farm occupations required baskets, and this need was met by two basket makers, using osiers which grew west of the Bridge. There are still two men in the town restoring antique furniture by hand, but at the time we are considering two cabinet makers and two chairmakers had businesses here.

The home brewing industry was supplied with barrels by two coopers. Twenty-two named houses were listed as 'victuallers' and there were four inns. Obviously, they all supplied alcoholic drinks, brewed from malt supplied by the four maltsters.

Two coachmaking concerns carried on their manufacturing in the town. The coach trade required specified wood for the various parts. The panels and casings were fir deal with mahogany floors and ash was used for the frames. The wheels, a specialist job, were made of beech or ash for the felloes, and oak or elm for the spokes. Leather was used as a covering for the foreboot and the mail boxes.

The professional classes were also represented. The customs and excise had their representative at the stamp office in the *Old Red Lion*. After the Bank of England was founded in 1694 other London banks had representatives in various towns. Horden, Molineux and Bishton of Newport drew on Harcourt, Blake, Sanson, Postlethwaite and Tamar, No. 65 Lombard Street, London.

One of the institutions in an English rural settlement is the 'pub' and, even in towns today, 'the local' is part of the environment. In 1485 the hospitality of the town must have been stretched to breaking point when Henry Tudor passed through with 5,000 men on his way to the battle of Bosworth where he defeated Richard III to become Henry VII. They had camped at Pave Lane on Muster Hill, a name which survives to this day.

The Justices of the Peace were given power to supervise and, if necessary, suppress the numbers of alehouses in the Licensing Statute of 1495 and in 1552 all sellers of ale were required to have the licence. It became customary for these houses to adopt a name. Although over a hundred named houses have been listed in Newport and neighbourhood, the highest number at one time was 33 in 1840 which had dropped to 16 by 1926.

The sale of wine was causing the government some concern and an Act was passed in 1553 limiting the number of taverns allowed in towns. Shrewsbury was allowed three and there is a record of a 'Vintner in St Marye Street', Newport, in 1597.

Brewster Sessions were inaugurated in 1736, at which the justices of the peace would issue licences to 'fit and proper persons' authorising them to keep inns, alehouses and victualling houses. In 1789 Barfoot and Wilkes list 25 victuallers, all in named houses. By 1822 (Pigott's directory) the list shows four inns, 23 taverns and public houses, and two liquor merchants.

The Beerhouse Act of 1830 enabled 'any householder assessed to poor rate, on payment of two guineas a year, to sell beer by retail in his dwelling house for consumption on or off the premises'. This was 'deemed expedient for the better supplying of the public with beer in England to give greater facilities for the sale thereof than are at present afforded by licences to keepers of inns, alehouses and victualling houses'. Probably, this accounted for the nine beer retailers along with two inns, two taverns and 20 public houses to be found in Newport in 1840, according to Robson's directory.

The Refreshment Houses Act (1860) made provision for the licensing of refreshment houses not already licensed as alehouses or beerhouses, and may be the reason for the change in description to nine inns and eight public houses, with

28. Cooper making a barrel.

29. Account for purchase of wines, 1828.
(by permission of Mr. Brian Williams).

30. Advertisement for Elkes'
Dining and Tea Rooms

only five beer retailers in 1870. The situation was unchanged in Newport until the introduction of the 'six day' and 'early closing' licences (1904) which were introduced to halt the serious social and other problems of the late 19th century. By 1900, Henry Elkes the baker had added a Temperance Hotel to the list, and the Salopian Aerated Water Manufacturers had a place in the town. Earlier in 1885, a Mr. John Davenport (no relation to the well-known name), a ginger beer manufacturer, had his shop in the High Street.

There were numerous maltsters in the town supplying the small brewers, but the water was not good enough to encourage a large scale industry. The Newport (Salop) Brewery Co. Ltd. was malting and brewing in the early part of the century in the buildings now occupied by John Ruisling Ltd., but by the First World War they had stopped brewing, and in fact used the plant to make jam from fruit supplied by local growers. The buildings were then used by a corn merchant who also had a shed in the canal wharf. Home-brewing was carried out in Newport in this century using the old-fashioned copper, 'a bushel of malt, a pound of hops, 4 lbs. of dark brown sugar, ½ lb. of yeast or balm, 10 gallons of water'.

The change in the role that the licensing trade has played in the life of Newport parallels the change in the town itself. From a predominantly agricultural community with a passing trade, it has developed into an urban market town with 12 houses for 9,000 inhabitants as against 26 for 2,000 inhabitants at the end of the 18th century.

31. Brewing beer on the hearth.

VI

NOVA BURGA

The coat of arms in the Council Offices bears the name 'Nova Burga', 'new borough'. This, of course, comes from Newport being a borough town, a status which gives the town the right to have a mayor. In 1801, according to the National Census of England, Newport had a population of 2,307 inhabitants. By 1851 the number had risen to 2,906. The national figure, by contrast, had risen from an estimated six million in 1700 to nine million in 1801 and 21 million in 1851. How do we relate the small increase in Newport with the national expansion? This could be quite easily understood except for the increase in the industries which appeared in the town in the same period while the traditional services continued at the same level. We have other indications that the town, although small, was a prosperous one and of importance in the locality.

Three directories, for 1822, 1840 and 1850, present an interesting picture, although they do not present the full story, and leave us with questions which we will try to answer here and elsewhere. The first question is why so many industries started in the town, and the second, why the population did not expand as it did in other towns? We will consider the types of industries and why they did not lead to an expansion in the population.

By 1840 (Robson's directory) the canal had come to the town, cutting costs of transport by 75 per cent., and providing a convenient way of importing bulky raw materials. The importation of strong flax and hemp from abroad had made it possible to make stronger ropes and now that the opportunity had come to bring the raw material into the town, a rope maker set up in the 'walk', running from St Mary Street to Tan Bank, which was still in use at the close of the century.

Boughey and Allkins had 'the principal manufactory (one of a truly ingenious and interesting character) from which all kinds of bendware and various turnery, together with hair sieves, and dairy requisites of every kind are produced, of the most perfect and approved description. A manufactory for agricultural implements and a considerable iron and brass foundry are also in the town'. A brick and tile maker operated in Water Lane. These are all operations which benefit from a supply of cheap coal available on the canal from the Stafford coal field. This coal was also necessary for the gas works, which had been set up in the town.

By 1850 an umbrella maker and gun and pistol maker were added to the clock and watch makers, while a clog maker (using alder trees) started a business, no doubt

W. S. UNDERHILL

respectfully solicits orders for

CAST-IRON LAND ROLLERS,

fitted with Wrought-iron Frames, very strong and durable ;

BALANCE LEVER HORSE RAKES,

the most simple and lowest pric'd Article in the Trade ;

WROUGHT-IRON CULTIVATORS,

the strongest yet lightest in use ;

PATENT PLOUGHS,

with cast Shares, for strong and light lands ;

RIDGE OR MOULDING PLOUGHS,

with newly-invented expanding apparatus ;

TURNIP SEED DRILLS,

either with front wheel or shafts.

For further Particulars and Prices, see his Catalogue, which will be forwarded in reply to post-paid applications.

W. S. U. wishes to return many thanks to his numerous Friends for their very liberal encouragements, and assures them no trouble on his part shall be spared to merit their continued support.

Notwithstanding the high price of iron, the prices of many of his Implements have been but slightly advanced, and several important Improvements made.

Implement Works,
Newport, Shropshire, March 1st, 1853.

T. G. ICKE, PRINTER, NEWPORT.

32. Advertisement for W. S. Underhill Implement Works.

exporting his wares to Lancashire and Yorkshire mill workers. A change in drinking habits might be inferred by the appearance of a soda water manufacturer and tea and spirit dealers on the lists of retailers.

Whether the pool which had by now disappeared, had been used for fish or not, we find a fishmonger and game dealer with their shops in the town. The tradition of families following the same occupations through succeeding generations seemed to be changing slightly in that although there was an increase in new occupations the rise in population in the town compared with the growing towns was much smaller.

If we look at three specimen families connected with Newport from 1789 until 1885, we get some idea of how the number of activities in the town increased, but

	SILLITOE	*SYLVESTER*	*ICKE*
1789	Cheesemonger Butcher Victualler Innkeeper, *The Crown*		Grocer Stationer Baker
1822	Victualler Inkeeper, *The Crown* Baker	Bookseller Printer Stationer Commissioner for taking bail Manufacturer of composition roller for inking metal types Post Office	Cooper Druggist Grocer Innkeeper, *Raven and Bell* Maltster Timber Merchant Bendware Carriers
1840	Boarding and day school Baker *The Crown* (sold)	Bookseller Printers Postmaster Shropshire Bank Co.	Cooper Grocer Druggist
1850	Baker Confectioner Post Office Stamp Office	Shropshire Bank Co. Savings Bank Musical Instrument sellers Dealer of Patent medicines Account Book Manuf. Religious Tract Society	Grocers Tea Dealer Hop Merchant Seed Merchant Fertilizer Merchant
1856	Postmistress	Shropshire Bank Co. Publisher of *Newport Advertiser* Booksellers Stationers Printers Bookbinders Dealer in Patent Medicines	Chemist Druggist Grocer Draper Printer Booksellers Stationers Engraver
1870	Young Ladies' School	NONE	Stationer Newsagent
1885	NONE	NONE	NONE

not the population which we might expect, and also the rise and fall of the impact of families in a community.

With better roads and improved coaches journeys became much quicker and by 1822 the new post coach (*The Sovereign*) ran from London to Birmingham in 14 hours with connections for Shrewsbury, Chester and Holyhead. Coaches going to Liverpool left from the *Crown Hotel*, London, every day with connections for Shrewsbury and Stafford from the *Victoria Hotel*, St Mary Street, Newport. The *Aurora* ran to Birmingham through Wolverhampton on Monday, Wednesday and Friday from the *White Horse*, Newport. There were also 16 coaches from London to Chester daily passing through the town, plus carriers' waggons to Birmingham and Chester from the *King's Arms*. Working with the canal, a waggon left the *Wharf Tavern* on Tuesday and Thursday for Shifnal, Madeley, Ironbridge and other destinations.

By 1840 regular coach services to Birmingham, Liverpool, Shrewsbury and Stafford were in operation from Newport, as were carriers of goods from the canal to Albrighton, Birmingham, Shifnal and Stafford. Mr. Sylvester had a weekly delivery to Stone which met 'the London, Liverpool, Manchester and North Carriers both by land and water'.

The itinerant merchants attending the markets and fairs, the growth of the iron industry in Coalbrookdale, mining at Oakengates and the Great Road from London carrying the traffic to Chester must all have had an influence on the economy and growth of Newport. They also had a deteriorating effect on the Newport Division of the turnpiked road. This made it necessary for the trustees to ask for an increase in the tolls, as they had 'expended more than the Tolls granted and now a considerable sum is due'. This was 'by reason of the great and heavy carriage upon the said Newport Division of Road, also the distance of the materials imported fit or proper for the repair thereof and the inadequacy of the Tolls granted'. They had been using 200 tons of Clee Hill Dhu stone annually but were also interested in Cerriog granite from Chirk and Rowley Stone from Dudley if the cost of transport was favourable.

They were allowed to charge 'for any carriage drawn by horse or mule, ox, steer or bull, not in pairs, 4d. if the wheels were over 6 in. wide, but 6d. if narrower; for any carriage drawn by ox, steer or bull drawing in pairs abreast 3d., if less than 6 in. the charge was 4½d., horse or mule laden or unladen, not drawing, 1½d.'. The broad wheels spreading the load did not

33. Carrier with waggon.

cut the road as badly as the narrow wheels and were therefore charged at a lesser rate. Any ass laden or unladen, possibly lighter on the road than a horse, was charged 1s. A drove of oxen, cows or neat (milk) cattle paid 1s. 3d. per score while a drove of calves, pigs, sheep or lambs was 10d. a score.

In 1864 an account of the Newport, Ternhill turnpike road showed that the increased tolls had made the business more profitable: expenses amounted to £179 11s. Even so, this road ceased to be turnpiked in 1867.

The surveying and reports on the roads were of sufficient importance to warrant the applicants stating their credentials at the county assizes:

SALOP LENT ASSIZES 1810

W. Atkins of Kinstock Common Salop, Yeoman 53 years and Thos. Cadman Swarley make Oath that for upwards of 9 years last employed by the Commissioners as the Surveyor of the Turnpike road leading from Newport in the said County towards Eccleshall in the County of Stafford and this dept.

Thos. Cadman is now surveyor of the Turnpike road leading from Newport towards Coventry upon which road he hath been employed for 20 years.

It appears to them to be partially but insufficiently repaired and is so full of Holes and Rutes in various parts as to be extremely perilous to all persons and Carriages, and cannot in their judgement be put into good and lasting repair at less expense than 1,000£.

The inspectors of the resulting repairs were obliged to submit a Certificate of Magistrates of Roads in Repair, written on parchment.

We Ralph Leede Esq. and the Rev. Rob. Outlaw two of His Majesty's Justices of the Peace acting in and for the County of Salop, do hereby certify that we have this day viewed a certain common and ancient King's Highway in the Township of Chetwynd in the parish of Chetwynd in the said County leading from Newport to the said County to Whitchurch in the same County beginning at Chetwynd End and ending at Stanford Bridge containing in length 6,900 yds. or thereabouts and in breadth 30 ft. now under indictment in the Court of Assizes for the said County and that the same hath been well and sufficiently gravelled and is now in good and substantial order and repair and likely so to continue. And we further certify that we have not either of us any messuage, lands, Tenements, Tithes situate or arising within ye said Township, nor any Estate or Interest therein, witness our Hands this 14th day of May in the year of our Lord 1813.

The roads up to 1862 had been the responsibility of each parish, but as the result varied so much in different parishes, Highway Boards were formed by an act to regularise the maintenance of important roads and gradually took over all parish roads and most of the turnpike roads. Under local government acts the county councils became responsible for main roads in 1889, and in 1894 the rural district councils for local roads.

The state of the roads encouraged tradesmen to look for alternative means of transport. One primitive means had been to use rivers. Specially-constructed canals had been developed for the carriage of goods on the Continent. In England the River Severn had from Roman times been an obvious method of transporting the products of the Midlands to Bristol and the sea. 'The King's High Stream of the Severn' had been free of tolls to the king's subjects, which helped the industrial Midlands in competition with foreign traders, but getting the goods to the boats, especially bulky products, was a difficult and expensive task. Another problem was in moving the barges upstream, but in 1531 Henry VIII permitted haulage by gangs of men and by 1811 there was a continuous horse-towing path along the Severn.

The lessons learned on the Severn made landowners look to the rivers on their estates for the carriage of heavy goods. The greater use of horses and carriages meant it was possible to export bulky feeding stuff off the farm and to import new fertilisers. The growing importance of coal as a supply of industrial energy and fuel for heating homes was perhaps the biggest motivation for those landowners who were fortunate enough to have deposits on their estates. However, the cheapness and ease of water transport was obvious: a load of three tons was the maximum weight on a wagon, whilst 12 tons could be carried on a barge. Once the horse had been taught to 'hang in the collar' in order to get the barge started, it could move the heavier load with less effort than on the road. It was found that mules, although harder to train, possessed good staying power, working harder and living longer than horses.

The first canal system to benefit Newport was the Donnington Wood Canal and its branches. Earl Gower, the owner of much land — Donnington Wood, Wrockwardine Wood and Ketley — was inspired by the success of his brother-in-law, the Duke of Bridgewater, who had built the famous Worsley-Manchester canal in 1761, to start canal-building in 1765. The part of the system which became known locally as the Duke of Sutherland's Canal connected the coal and ironstone workings with the mines at Lilleshall to their output at Pave Lane. An entry in Bagshaw's directory of 1851 says that 'this canal in use from 1782, almost wholly supplies the town with very superior coal varying in price from 6s. 3d. to 10s. 10d. ton'.

Thomas Telford, a famous canal engineer, was to have a great effect on Newport. In 1795 William Clowes, who was cutting a canal from Trench to Shrewsbury, died and Telford, who had had many achievements both in England and Scotland, was asked to finish the work. He was asked to engineer a canal to link Birmingham with Liverpool 'with collateral branches'. One of these branches was the Norbury-Newport branch, which joined with the Trench-Shrewsbury canal at Wappenshall.

In 1830, the Birmingham to Liverpool Junction Canal Company opened negotiations in Newport to 'buy the whole piece of land offered to them at £180 per acre' with the proviso that 'the company be directed to bring up the level of the Brook from below the Bridge at Chetwynd End, and to lay a culvert under the canal into the old course so as to drain the land' (Newport Mere). This was eventually done.

One of the difficulties Telford had to overcome was dropping the level from the 300 feet contour at Norbury, using 15 locks in two miles, and building a reservoir to replace the water used by them. Telford had mastered the cut-fill system where the spare solid from the cuts was used in the necessary embankments. This number of locks was one of the reasons for the canal falling into disuse, and a major obstacle to reopening it for pleasure craft.

One problem was making the canal watertight to stop the water filtering through to the surrounding area. This was done 'by a mixture of well tempered clay and sand reduced to a semi-fluid state and rendered impervious to water by manual labour, as by working and chopping it about with spades. It is usually applied in three or more strata to a thickness of about three feet, each stratum being united with the one beneath. Over the top course a layer of common soil is laid. Only careful puddling stops the water leaking'. A few years ago, when cleaning out the wharf basin a 'JCB' driver unwittingly nearly broke the seal before he was stopped.

A tremendous number of men, compared with present day construction, was needed for these operations. This force was supplied mostly by the immigrant population of Irish 'navvies'. The canals had become known as navigations and the workers as 'navvies', a name which later came to be applied to the early road and railway construction workers. When the canal was being built through Newport, over seventy men were listed on the 1811 census returns as working on the canal.

When making the canal, the pool was used as a basin, two wharves being constructed for the barges and the carriers, with a system of feeder routes on the road being operated from these wharves. In 1822, Mr. Sylvester had a carrier service leaving the town every week . . . 'meets the London, Liverpool, Manchester and North Carriers both by land and water'. It was possible to send goods to London by water from Newport in 1840 using the choice of three carriers on Monday, Tuesday, Thursday or Saturday. These were Pickford, Crowley & Co., with the *Neptune Conveyance*, and Hanshall & Co., whose coach left the *Wharf Tavern* on Tuesday and Thursday, returning in the afternoon. By 1850, the Shropshire Union Railway and Canal Co. had their own wharf on the canal, while Pickfords and Hanshall used Ward's Wharf.

An interesting feature on the canal is the Skew Bridge near Forton, where the road, river and canal intersected. The sketch shows how Telford overcame this difficulty.

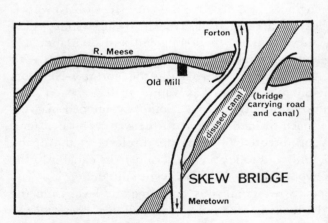

He also remade the town bridge with an arch for the canal and one for the Strine. One of the buildings on the wharf is still used by the council for their Leisure and Community equipment, while the other was taken to Blists Hill Museum, where it now houses the woodworking exhibit.

The canal effectively removed the remnants of the pool through which it was constructed. Today, however, three lengths of the canal have been preserved and stocked with fish, and the surroundings

34. Sketch map of Skew Bridge and Canal.

landscaped, a gesture perhaps to the pool which played such a part in the original settlement.

With the advent of the canal, the goods trade was transferred to the water, the canal being used by three carriers to London on Tuesday, Thursday and Saturday, and three other carriers to Liverpool daily. The two posting houses and stage coaches were still in operation on the roads. An agent for the combined railway and canal carriage trade continued in business until 1926 when the canal was closed.

The railways were at first in competition for the passenger trade carried by the stage coaches and canal 'packets' (passenger barges), but they soon realised the potential of the goods traffic carried by the canals. In the three years (1845–47) 948 miles of national waterways fell into railways hands and in 1846 the Shropshire Union Railway and Canal Co. bought the Newport canal. By 1850, the railway was running from Stafford to Wellington through Newport.

This railway was itself later bought by the London and Northwestern Railway which was in turn absorbed by the L.M.S. The L.N.W.R. operated their own fleet of boats, using them as heavy short-haul feeders for the railway.

35. Millward's bakery and shop at the Canal.

The stage coaches tried to cope with the threat of the railways by lowering fares and acting as feeders in areas which were not covered by rail, but their days· were numbered. In Newport by 1850 there is no mention of coaches, but the Shropshire Union Railway was running daily to Shrewsbury and Wellington, and also 'conveying by water to London, Birmingham and Wolverhampton and forward to all parts of England from their wharf twice a week. To Manchester, Liverpool, Chester and Montgomeryshire from their wharf twice a week'.

By 1856, Pickfords were not using the canal, but advertised as 'by railway' and from then onwards the same agent handled all traffic on both the railway and the canal. It was not in the interest of the railways to keep up the canals so they raised the canal tolls and prohibited Sunday work until, as the trade declined, the Newport canal effectively ceased as a trade route in 1929.

We think of the stage coach, the canal and the railway as following one after the other, but in fact they did overlap in time, stimulating and competing with one another until the railway emerged victorious.

In the *Journal of the Royal Agricultural Society*, no. 19, we read that 'in the Wrekin there is a fair proportion of grassland of good quality near the Tern and Strine, also near Cherrington and Lee Brooks. Few districts can produce a better collection of improved implements than the one now under notice'.

Although agriculture suffered a setback after the Napoleonic Wars, it did not deter agricultural implement makers from setting up in Newport. One of the main features of agricultural progress in the 19th century was the introduction of the reaping machine, followed by that of the threshing drum. The importation from abroad of ammoniacal and phosphatic manures not only helped the yield of crops but built up a fertility which enabled farmers to modify the four-course system if they wished. Overseas sources of protein (oil cake, cotton cake etc.) made it possible to carry more cattle per acre and have better finished products, either beef or milk.

The drainage of the valley continued to be a problem with the Weald Moors a block to the outfall of the Tern, where several mills had kept the level high to ensure enough

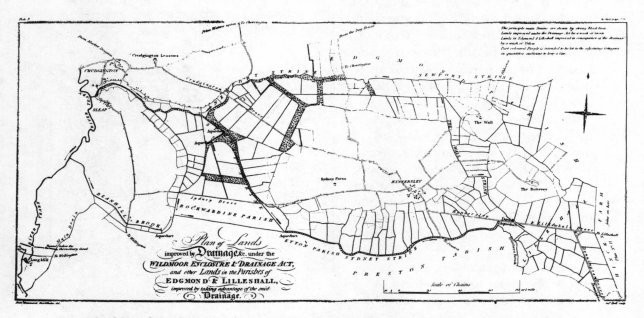

36. Map of the drainage scheme carried out at the instigation of the Duke of Sutherland.

water to operate the wheels. It was not until the early 19th century that the Marquess of Stafford, later the Duke of Sutherland, carried out an intensive drainage scheme. A description of the work done, by hand labour, shows that the task was a formidable one.

> On the Lilleshall estate there has been excavated about seventeen thousand yards of embankment, twenty seven thousand yards of water courses deepened and scoured; forty-six thousand yards of main ditches made or deepened; three hundred and fifteen thousand yards of fence ditches deepened, scoured and straightened. Forty-nine thousand yards of old fence stocked; thirty thousand yards of new quick (hawthorn) fences made; twenty thousand yards of turf draining, and four hundred and sixty-two thousand yards of underground draining, laid with tiles and filled with stones.

A monument was erected on Lilleshall Hill in memory of the Duke.

Newport had its own powers and methods of dealing with misdemeanours; the Newport Patrol, with their headquarters in what was once the Booth Hall, consisted of 12 members who had the job of policing the town in four-hour shifts each night. When the market house was demolished in 1859 the town stocks were removed with it. They had been used for many years as an entry in the *Shrewsbury Chronicle* of 1785 shows:

37. The pillory, Newport.

Yesterday at the Quarter Sessions for this town and liberties Elizabeth Morris aged 72 convicted of falsely accusing John Maddon with an assault on Mary Gregory aged 14 years (with an intent to extort money from him, the said John Maddon) was ordered to stand in the pillory this day, to be imprisoned for six months, and to find sureties for her good behaviour for seven years.

The surrounding countryside had to enforce the law itself in many ways. One example of how seriously this was taken is the following contract with a gamekeeper:

Know all men that the Colonel Fenton Boughey Esq. Lord of the Manor of Forton and Coley etc. hereby nominate, authorise, and appoint Robert Bayley of Aqualate within the said Manor, to be my Gamekeeper of within and upon (the said Manor) with full power, licence and authority to kill and take any pheasant, partridge, fish and other game whatever in and upon my said Manor for my sole use and immediate benefit and also to take and seize all such guns, bows, Setting Dogs, pointers, spaniels, Lurchers and other dogs. To note Trammels, Sowbells, Hays and other such pipes, snares and other Engines for the taking and killing of carrion, Pheasant, Partridges and other game and also all manner of fishing acts, angles, Leaches, Pitchers, willy lines and other devices, instruments and Engines for the taking and killing of fish as within my said Manor or used or employed by any persons who by Law are prohibited to keep or use the same.

Given under my hand and Seal the 26th day of October in the Year of our Lord 1808.

J.F.B.

The local farmers were often dissatisfied with the apprehension and punishment of offenders, as the *Articles for the Forton Association for the Prosecution of Felony* shows:

Whereas divers Burglaries, Robberies, Larcenies and other Felonies and divers misdemeanors are frequently committed whereof many persons are put to great trouble and Expense in recovering or seeking after their property. And in persecuting the offender for want of sufficient and speedy assistance have often escaped from or eluded Justice to the Encouragement of such Crimes and the great injuring and Vexation of the County.

Now for the preventing the like offences and for the more effectual and expeditious pursuit, apprehension and vigorous prosecution thereof, we do severally covenant and agree to form ourselves into a Society for the detection and prosecution of all felonies and misdemeanors which shall be committed on our or any of our persons or property to be known by the name 'Forton Association'.

FOURTH   That every member shall keep an account of the age, colour, height and marks of every Horse, Mare, Gelding or Colt in his or her possession in Order that a full description thereof may be given to the persons who shall be appointed to pursue them . . .

LASTLY   That the true performance . . . of each every clause and article and resolution and agreement to be hereafter made pursuant to hereto according to the true Spirit, Intent and Meaning We each and every one do bind ourselves with the Trustees of the said Society for this purpose only in the sum of Ten Pounds . . . subscribed our names the Tenth Day of September in the Year of Our Lord 1806.

The waste of water in the town caused a great deal of concern. Some of the households and the public houses had their own wells, but in general the supply had remained unchanged since 1300. In 1813, a committee had been formed to 'consider what improvement may be made in the resources and works of the Corporation for bringing and distributing the water through the Borough'. In the original scheme, the water was fed into six open cisterns in the High Street, but as rubbish was continually being thrown into them by children and a person had drowned in one of them, the burgesses decided to close them and put hydrants in their place from which the 'inhabitants drew water gratuitously'. In 1817 an order enabled 'any inhabitant of the town of Newport to be allowed, on applying to the Bailiff, to carry a pipe half an inch in diameter from the main pipe for the supply of their houses on paying the sum of fifteen shillings annually'. A consequence of this was that it was estimated that one quarter of the whole supply was being lost from ill-constructed water closets which had no self-acting valves. In spite of a warning that the bailiffs were instructed to cut off the supply of wrongdoers, 'a great deal of loss was still suffered from imperfect fittings and carelessness of servants in leaving taps running to waste. A very certain remedy for this objectionable state would be the adoption of the metre system. In Glasgow, for instance, as much as 30 gallons per head of the whole population had been saved'. In addition to the loss of water, Mr. Massey, the Water Superintendent, complained of the noise of 'air in the pipes through the night'.

In 1856 it was decided to introduce piped water throughout the town. A declaration with 60 signatures states that:

We the undersigned owners or occupiers of Houses in the Town of Newport agree with the present Bailiffs of the Corporation, that such as have not already laid down pipes for the purpose hereinafter mentioned will at our own expense cause to be laid down, three-quarter pipes from the main waterpipe of Newport Waterworks and to pay the said Bailiffs, an annual sum or rental.

An agreement with owners or occupiers of houses for renting water at 10d. in the £1 on poor relief rate was reached, the Corporation offering to fix a three-quarter inch socket in the main pipe.

When workmen were digging a trench for water pipes into Salter's Lane they found the remains of an old oak post. This was in the position for the upright to the bar which was raised and lowered as a toll bar, the 'Lowrie Bar' as it was called. Near the same spot a curious brass weight was found, similar to the one illustrated here. The three lions and three lilies in quarters were the royal arms of France and England and it is thought to date from the time of Edward III whose edict standardised the weights and measures 'throughout the realm of England'. It measured six by four and a half inches, by one and three-quarter inches thick, and weighed seven and a half pounds. It was obviously shaped for hanging, and may have been carried by officials checking weights and measures, or by the toll men assessing goods for toll charges into the town.

Responsibility for the water supply was transferred to the Newport (Salop) Market Company providing:

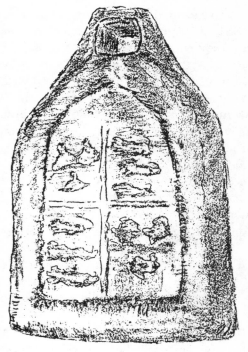

38. Brass weight found at 'Lowrie Bar'. (From F. J. Jones, *Trans. Shrop. Arch. Soc.*)

1. The Company laid down a three quarter inch pipe to the main, on payment of an annual rent of £2.
2. The water shall at all times be applicable in the first place to the supply of the common conduits of the town and in the case of fire.
3. No unnecessary waste of water.

The Bridge Terrace was supplied with water in 1873 and in 1876 it was extended from Stafford Street by two new branches to Stafford Road and the Marsh Lane. It was not until 1881 that the supply reached Audley Avenue, Wellington Road, New Street and Beaumaris Lane.

The land in which the Walls Head spring was situated was in the possession of Ralph Leeke of Longford. In an agreement between Mr. Leeke and the High Steward, Deputy Steward, Bailiffs and burgesses of Newport, the latter were given 'a licence to let from year to year, all or so much as the burgesses think proper of the land at Church Aston adjoining the reservoir and Baddeley's Wells demised by the Leekes to the burgesses by an indenture of 21st May last, 1878. No Horse, Cow, Bull, Bullock, Heifer or Pig to be turned onto the land, which is only to be mowed or grazed by sheep'. The freehold of this land was obtained by the burgesses in 1885 for £800. Following the 1875 Public Health Act, the local sanitary board had 'invested itself with the powers to take over the water supply and hydrants'.

In view of the hard winters experienced recently, it is interesting to note a report of 1881 that 'the intense frost of last year has damaged some pipes, and therefore these are requiring repair bills'. An examination of the supply lines in 1885 'found that the joints of the cast iron spigot and socket mains instead of being made in the usual way with lead run into the sockets and well cauked, were said to be only made with Gaskin Yarn, plastered on the outside with Roman Cement so that while the cast iron pipes would be capable of sustaining an internal working pressure of 300 ft. head of water it was apprehended that the joints would not sustain a head of more than thirty feet'. The surveyor commented: 'Considering the length of time that these pipes have been laid down, I look upon the results of the examination as speaking volumes for the extraordinary purity of your supply'.

A massive reorganisation of the water supply took place in 1894. Baddeley's well was sunk to a depth of 100 feet and fitted with a strong, deep well pump made at Mr. Massey's foundry in the town, powered by two Ruston Hornsby's Ackroyd paraffin engines. A system of three-inch and seven-inch iron pipes was laid down with appropriate sluice valves and fire hydrants fed from a new 150,000 gallon service reservoir.

Entertainment was well catered for in the early 19th century, as this petition shows:

PETITION FOR A LICENCE TO PLAY IN NEWPORT

To the worshipful Justices of the Peace at the quarter sessions of the Peaceholders at Shrewsbury in the County of Salop on the Eleventh Day of May 1814.

The Humble petition of Shanton of Burton-upon-Trent in the County of Stafford.

Shows that your petitioner hath with the approbation of the Inhabitants of the Town of Newport in the County of Salop erected at a considerable Expense within this town a commodious Theatre for the performance of such Tragedies, Comedies, Operas, Plays or Farces as are acted shall be represented at the patents on Licensed Theatre in all access or prescribed by Law have been submitted to the Inspection of the Lord Chamberlain.

Your petitioner therefore prayeth that your Worships will be pleased to grant him a License for such performance and within the Town parish of Newport aforesaid for a period of 60 days from the First Day of March next.

This theatre was held in what had been the original Wesleyan church. Later in 1873, we find Mr. Liddle recording in his diary:

Tickets for amateur theatricals . . . . £1 5s. 0d.
Tickets for theatricals . . . . 4s. 0d.

For those interested in using the circulating library the following titles were available in 1829:

1   *Cambria Triumphous, or Britain in its Perfect Lustre*
2   *Travels in Ceylon*
3   *Secret Correspondence of Madame le Maintenon* (3 vols.)
4   *Memoirs of Casanova* (3 vols.)
5   *Gymnastics* by 'Clias'

6   Grosse's *Classical Dictionary of the Vulgar Tongue*
7   Clark on *Natural and Artificial Teeth*
8   *Act of Preserving the Hair, with Curious Recipes for Oils, etc.*
9   Taylor's *Complete Weather Guide*
10 *Elements of Morality*
11 *Converts from Infidelity* (2 vols.)

NOVELS AND ROMANCES

12 *Anselmo, a Tale of Italo* (2 vols.)
13 *Actress, or Countess and No Countess, A Novel* (2 vols.)

DIVINITY

14 Blair's *Sermons and Life*
15 Willison's *Afflicted Man's Companion*

POETRY AND DRAMA

16 *False Delicacy, Word to the Wise, School for Rakes, Brothers*

JUVENILE LIBRARY

17 *English History (on a new plan)*
18 Fergusson's *Astronomy*
19 *Economy of Human Life*
20 Enfield's *Natural Theology*
21 *Experiments in Chemistry*

In 1861, in the preface of his *Lives of the Engineers*, Samuel Smiles commented on the previous hundred years: 'England was regarded principally as a magazine for the supply of raw materials. . . . After the lapse of a century, we find the state of things has become entirely reversed. Instead of borrowing engineers from abroad we now send them to all parts of the world. We have completed a magnificent system of canals, turnpike roads, bridges and railways, by which the internal communications of the country have been completely opened up'. Although this may not apply to Newport in particular nevertheless the revolution in the nation was reflected in the development of the town with the canal, the turnpike roads and its various industries.

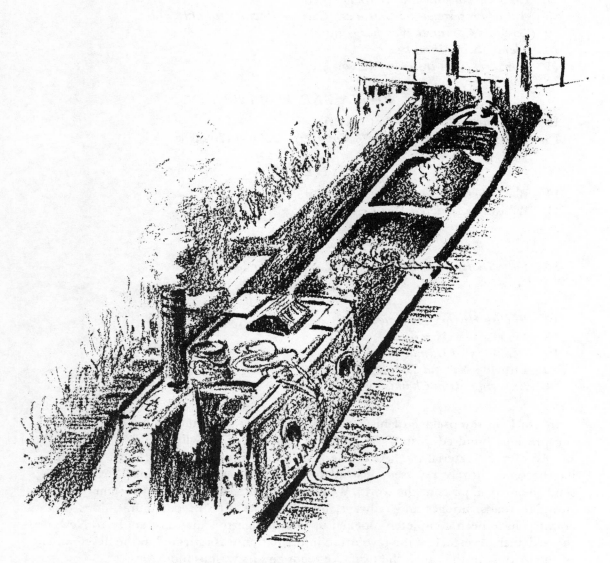

39. Canal long-boat in a lock.

VII

NEWPORT, SALOP

Writing in *My Shropshire Days on Common Ways* Mr. John Beard, C.B.E., says of Newport: 'To those of us who lived West of the Tern in the later part of the 19th century it was almost an unknown place, due to its market being secondary to Shrewsbury, Wellington and Market Drayton. It has never had great ambitions although it has the widest street of any town in Shropshire'.

This may very well be borne out by the slow growth in population but, on the other hand, in the 19th century one senses a change to a more urban outlook. It continued to supply the traditional services for travellers and supplies for local people, but new industries in the town matched a changing lifestyle in the nation. The leather trade was well represented with both saddles and harness manufacturers for horses, and boot and shoe makers for their riders. Wood was still extensively used by carpenters and carriage makers, and the fashioning of wood by turners and bendware manufacturers continued. The household furniture makers were joined by upholsterers, a business which is carried on in a small way in the town today.

By 1856, according to the *Post Office Directory*, a section of metalworking within the traditional iron working of previous years had developed. By 1870, two foundries were actively engaged near the canal, in conjunction with agricultural implement makers, one of whom later started making one of the earliest bicycles as well as iron hurdles and fencing to replace the traditional wooden ones. Nail making and machine making were carried out in the town with the wheelwright and millwright plying their highly-skilled trades and there was also one man listed as a grinder. All of these industries still had an agricultural or rural connection.

A nurseryman, a gardener and seedsman, together with a potato dealer and a greengrocer, would suggest a need for more vegetables from householders who had no gardens, and perhaps more interest in the flower gardens of the bigger houses. By 1885, painters and house decorators appear for the first time. We also find two chimney sweeps. Perhaps these new trades mark the emergence of the 'middle class' in the town.

Naturally, as a service town, the appearance of different retailers is a logical occurrence. The clothing trade was moving away from the personal tailor and dressmaker, and led to ready-made clothes dealers and a baby linen warehouse. The presence of a rag merchant might be explained if he was collecting rags for the paper-making industry in Tibberton.

Ready-made Clothing and Outfitting

ESTABLISHMENT,

HIGH STREET, (near the Church), NEWPORT, Salop.

W. WIGGIN

Has now on hand a choice Stock of Boys', Youths', and Men's WINTER CLOTHING, consisting of Boys' and Youths' School Suits; Men's Coloured Doeskin Suits; also, a great variety of Coats, Trousers, and Vests, in newest styles and different patterns; Boys', Youths', and Men's Cord and Moleskin Jackets, Trousers, and Vests, also some choice things in Reefer Coats, OVERCOATS, and Waterproof Coats. Leather Leggings, COLOURED WOOLLEN SHIRTS, Umbrellas, Hats, Caps, Ties, Scarfs, Collars, Braces, &c. Boys', Youths', and Men's Worked Smock Frocks, Duck Slops and Jackets, and Painters' Overalls.

ANY ARTICLES EXCHANGED IF NOT APPROVED.

W.W. has also on hand a choice selection of Woollens, consisting of COATINGS, TROUSERINGS, &c., suitable for the present season.

Gentlemen's Garments made to order.

40. Advertisement for W. Wiggin, outfitter.

The age-old practice of keeping a pig and curing it for home use must have been disappearing as we now find pork butchers in the town. Although there were several hop merchants added to the maltsters, a coffee tavern appears.

We find the term 'estate agent' used for the first time, perhaps not as we know them today, and a lodging house in the High Street. Photography was a growing industry by 1870 and we find a photographer in the town and, perhaps an accompanying skill, an engraver. We also find a professor and teacher of music, and a commercial traveller had his residence there.

Clockmakers had their establishments in the town as early as the 17th century, many of then working with, or being the sons of, blacksmiths. The heavy machinery of the church clocks needed the blacksmiths, but as the demand grew for the smaller parts for grandfather clocks, and especially watches, the watchmakers, although qualified by apprenticeship in the manufacture of these parts, tended to rely on large-scale production elsewhere and bought and built the various parts into their timepieces, engaging a local cabinet maker to build the wooden cases for the grand-father clocks. There seems to have been a fair amount of movement of personnel among the clockmakers as any son who wanted to follow in his father's occupation went away to an apprenticeship and often settled away from his father's place of business. This meant many names disappearing from the town, but some have left a mark. At the riot of Newport, one of those who made a statement was Michael Orme, a watchmaker in the town, and in 1778–80 Thomas Benbow, watchmaker, was a baillie, although he later moved to London.

An interesting picture of a family connected with the watch-making industry is shown in the table on page 72.

By the end of the 19th century, Newport was the seat of local government for the surrounding area. His Grace the Duke of Sutherland was lord of the manor, and held court leets annually. The county court, established under the County Court Act of 1846, sat once a month in the Town Hall for the recovery of debts to

41. A grandfather clock.

any amount not exceeding £20. By the close of the century, the county court was sitting every two months with a judge and jury and also dealt with cases of bankruptcy.

The growth of the population over the 150 years from 1800 was very steady in comparison with the increase in the number of small industries. The first 50 years from 1801 show an increase of ten per cent. per year in the number of small businesses. During the following 50 years, however, when the population remained steady, the small industries died out, and a single larger one took their place.

Newport, keeping abreast with the times, had a circulatory library as early as 1789 and a newsroom for those wishing to see the newspapers. Printing and bookbinding were carried out in the town, and in 1851 the town had its own local newspaper published weekly. When printing licences were abolished and freedom given to the press in 1695 it opened up the way for national newspapers and the commercial press. In the 18th century, travellers both in this country and abroad were putting their experiences on paper, novelists and educationalists putting their ideas before those of the public who were able to read. By 1900 Bennion, Horne, Smallman & Co. Ltd. were printing and publishing the *Newport and Market Drayton Advertiser*, the *Stone and Eccleshal Advertiser*, *Shifnall and Oakengates Advertiser*, *The Pupil Teacher* and *The Scholarship Student*.

The value of advertising was represented in the town by a town crier who kept the inhabitants informed about latest developments; his daughter ran a bill-posting service!

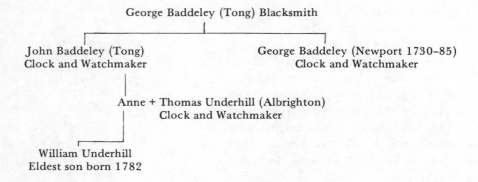

George Baddeley (Tong) Blacksmith

John Baddeley (Tong)   George Baddeley (Newport 1730–85)
Clock and Watchmaker   Clock and Watchmaker

Anne + Thomas Underhill (Albrighton)
Clock and Watchmaker

William Underhill
Eldest son born 1782

In 1822 in Newport listed as ironmonger and tinplate worker
1828–36 clock and watchmaker
1840 grocer, tallow chandler, ironmonger, brazier and tinplate worker
1850 in private residence in Church Aston
1850 brazier and tinplate worker, china and glass dealer, agricultural implement maker,
    ironmonger, nailmaker, tallow chandler

William Scott Underhill
1817–1884

1870 ironmonger, agricultural engineers, velocipede manufacturer
1900 Mrs. Underhill, 38 St Mary Street
    Executors — W. Underhill, Engineers, 38 St Mary Street

Robert Scott Underhill   John Scott Underhill
Ironmonger, 15 High Street   Clerk to U.D.C.

Letters have been used for centuries, either sent by special messengers or committed to travellers hoping that they would reach their destination. For those who were not able to write, scribes were employed and in Newport a writing master plied his trade. A sufficiency of stationers in the town made sure that the materials for writing were available. As the stage coach routes developed they supplied a method of transporting the letters. The local letters from Newport were sent by horse post in 1822 'meeting the London–Holyhead mail at Shifnal and the Manchester mail at the *Spread Eagle*', connecting with the post coaches, leaving in the morning at six and returning in the evening. Although Newport had a postal service in 1835, there were some towns in England of 12,000 people without a post office or a postman.

Before the establishment of the Penny Post in 1840, the cost of sending a letter from London to Ireland and getting an answer was one-fifth of the weekly wage of a labourer. The letter was costed by weight and paid for by the recipient. Rowland Hill suggested that letters be prepaid with a stamp at a cost of one penny for all distances. By 1860 the national post had increased in volume from 76 million to 642 million letters.

When the railway took over the mail, the letters 'arrived every morning at ½ past 7 and were despatched evening ¼ past six'. By 1856 letters were forwarded 'to all parts of England and Wales, there being two deliveries daily at 7.30 a.m. and 3.30 p.m. except Sundays when there was only one at 9 a.m. Money orders were granted and paid from 9 a.m. to 6 p.m. except Sundays'. The electric telegraph had been invented by Morse in 1832 and we find Mr. Liddle noting in 1877 that telegrams were 3s. 3d. The post office in the High Street had a telegraph service, supplied money orders and was a savings bank and insurance office. The night mail closed at 9.45 p.m. with extra halfpence stamps available up to 10 p.m.

By 1885, there was a wall box in Station Road cleared at 7 p.m. only, but the pillar box in the Upper Bar was cleared at 10.05 a.m. and 9 p.m. But by 1900 business was very brisk indeed, with a sub-post office opened in the Upper Bar with letters being 'despatched at 5.45 and 10.15 a.m., 12.30, 2.30 and 9.45 p.m. The wall box on the Station Road was cleared at 10 and 11 a.m., 2.15 p.m., 5 and 8.55 p.m.'. A parcel post and express delivery were also in operation.

The middle classes, seeking further education in order to fill the need for skilled engineering workers, founded institutes in various towns, one of which was established in Newport in 1851 as the Mechanics Institute, housed in the Town Hall.

The Newport Literary Institution was opened in 1883 at the corner of Wellington Road. It had reading, billiards, smoking and recreation rooms and a library of about two thousand volumes. It was removed in 1927 to its present position in the Town House in the High Street owned by the Boughey Trust.

One of the problems at the beginning of the 19th century had been the increase in the number of children caused by fewer of them dying under six years of age. The employment of children had led to Acts of Parliament, limiting the hours they were allowed to work, and later specifying how they were to be educated. Although there was no heavy industry in Newport, these educational reforms were to have an effect on the town.

In 1802 the Health and Morals of Apprentices Act ensured instruction of apprentices in the '3 Rs', and together with the Second Factory Act of 1819 set the age for starting work at nine years.

As we have seen, Newport could already boast of the Grammar School, the English School, apprenticeships and small private schools.

In the 1820 report of the Commissioner of Charities on the English School it was stated that 'This school has long been confirmed to the instruction of children in reading English and are taught to read well in the Bible. They are admitted on application to the headmaster, and remain as long as they please. The master receives his appointment by letters patent under the Great Seal'. In May 1820, there were between fifty and sixty pupils.

It is obvious that a good proportion of the working force could manage with no great degree of literacy. The craftsman apprentices, although benefiting from an ability to read, could soon master the vocabulary necessary for their jobs. Education, being parochial, was still church-controlled.

In 1841 in the Congregational Schoolroom in Wellington Road, a British school for infants was formed with 95 pupils. At the same time, a Sunday school with an attendance of 150 was started. An entry in the records of the Water Board in 1841 shows 'an application to have a pipe for water laid to the new school by the Chapel in Shrewsbury (Wellington) Road'.

The Anglican National Society founded a girls' National School in 1842 in Workhouse Lane for about seventy pupils. In 1869 the Marsh Trustees '. . . of this land, which is situate in the Avenue Road, formerly called Marsh Lane, gave about an acre for the site of the National School'. In 1870 a new National School was opened, incorporating the Girls' National School from Workhouse Lane (now called Schoolground Lane) and the infant school from Wellington Road. As the national society was Anglican, this was a Church of England school.

Foster's Act (1870) set up school boards in defined districts with the power to pass byelaws. Attendance at school was not universally compulsory, nor was education free (9d. per week) but free places could be obtained.

The establishment of the National School led, no doubt, to the falling off of attendance at the English School, which was by this time at the corner of Wellington Road, and it was sold by the Charity Commissioners in 1898, the headmaster being granted a pension for life. The investments from the sale are used today to give a yearly sum to apprentices to buy tools or text books. The stipulations are that they must be resident in Newport, a registered apprentice, and able to read a passage in English when appearing before the school board.

The infant section of the National School varied in size between 78 and 93 pupils, and in 1879 an inspector's report stated that 'The infants are in good order and have been taught with creditable success. I think the managers should now be prepared to build a new school'. The new infant school was built next to the junior school in 1899.

Various elementary education Acts enforced compulsory attendance, and in 1891 introduced government grants to replace school fees.

The fortunes of the Grammar school suffered a decline in the first half of the century, its roll falling to 59 pupils by 1850 and to only 32 pupils in 1860 (five in the upper school, 11 in the middle and 16 in the lower). By extending its catchment area to a five-mile radius, it had a larger roll in 1872, of 80 pupils (21 in the upper school, 22 in the middle and 37 in the lower school).

The result of the entrance examinations in the 1830s shows the extent of the catchment area and the varied occupations of the parents.

Entrance examination held Thursday 20th April, 1831

15 candidates   6 elected

AGE	RESIDENCE	PARENTS' OCCUPATION
13	Wilbrighton	Farmer
10	Church Aston	Maltster
11	Lilleshall	Keeper
11	Newport	Doctor
11	Lilleshall	Watchman
8	Newport	Tradesman

Examination held 10th August

13 Candidates   7 Elected

AGE	RESIDENCE	PARENTS' OCCUPATION
12	Market Drayton	Agent for coal wharf
11	Market Drayton	Agent for coal wharf
11	Edgmond	Solicitor
13	Preston (Weald Moors)	Threshing machine owner
8	Newport	Soldier
15	Donnington	Clergyman
14	Brockton	Farmer

There were 72 pupils in 1831, whose parents were all from Newport. They included a miner, solicitor, maltster, carrier, farrier, excise officer, surgeon, joiner, publican, sawyer, clerk to wool stapler, baker, blacksmith, pig dealer, plasterer, watchman, bricklayer, gardener, shoemaker, wheelwright, one farmer, grocer, and an attendant of lunatics — a truly varied assortment!

In 1838 the son of a Birmingham attorney, residing with his uncle in Newport, attended the grammar school. This is the first mention of boarders; one of the masters used a house in the High Street for this purpose. The places of residence of the boys' parents included Bury St Edmunds, Birmingham, Liverpool and Gloucester. In 1878 it became an aided school.

During the 19th century several small 'academies' appeared in Newport. These were private establishments catering for boarders, mostly girls. Miss Helen Bradbury had an establishment for ladies, boarding and day, at Chetwynd End in 1840. Miss Stevens and Miss Pritchard are also listed in local directories. Whether they had separate schools or assisted Miss Bradbury, who had moved to the High Street with a Miss Ann Guy, is not clear. In 1850 the Misses Atkinson and Cooke also ran a boarding and day school in the High Street.

John Sillitoe had a gentlemen's boarding and day school in the Old Hall in 1840, possibly assisted by Joseph Collier. In 1870 Miss Elizabeth and Mr. James Collier had a ladies' school in the High Street. James Pickin, schoolmaster in the English School, took over the Old Hall to conduct a classical and commercial school there until 1885. Jane Sillitoe had a young ladies' school in the High Street followed in 1885 by Miss Elizabeth Siderfin. By

Classical & Commercial School,

ASTON OLD HALL,

'NEWPORT, SALOP,

ESTABLISHED 1851,

AND CONDUCTED BY

MR. JAMES PICKIN.

——:o:——

TERMS ON APPLICATION.

42. Advertisement for Mr. Pickin's school.

1900, in Rosemount House, Miss Ashmore was giving modern and commercial education for girls with the inclusion of boys under seven years. Merevale College also accepted boys under seven years, together with girl boarders, preparing them for the Oxford local examinations.

When the English church separated from Rome, the Catholic form of worship continued to be maintained at Longford Hall, the seat of the Talbot family, until 1789 when George Wright, the priest in charge, moved to Salter's Hall.

This Hall was given by the Earl of Shrewsbury to the Vicar Apostolic of the Midland district and became the residence of the first Catholic Bishop of Shrewsbury until 1868. The present Roman Catholic Church, also a gift from the Earl, was built at Salter's Hall and was dedicated by Bishop Walsh, Vicar Apostolic of the Midland district. George Howe, the priest in charge from 1805 until 1832, was buried before the altar. In 1920 a large rose window with decorated tracery was installed in the west wall. In a niche is a statue of Our Lady and Child.

During the 16th century there is no record of the Anglican priests in Newport but in 1605 Richardus Felton was named as the rector. Apart from the years 1649–70, when three rectors were in charge, the average tenure of the incumbents to the present day has been 22 years.

We have already come across Nonconformism in the town in the 18th century, when Mr. Jones was expelled from Oxford. The chapel he built, somewhere behind Lloyd's Bank and the Grammar School, was being used as a schoolroom when Mr. Sylvester, a Congregational dissenter came as clerk to the Shropshire Banking Company (now Lloyd's Bank). He eventually purchased the building as an Independent chapel. This chapel 'was situate at the bottom and in a corner of the Bear Meadow, that lies at the back of the rectory, once the *Bear Inn*'.

As the congregation grew it was decided to build a new chapel and the present one in Wellington Road was opened in 1832, and the school and classrooms were added in 1841. This is now the United Reformed Church. (See Fig. 44, page 77).

The first licence (1797) for Wesleyan Methodist services in Newport was to enable them to be held in a house, but by 1813 the Shrewsbury circuit plan shows that Newport and Lilleshall were holding services on Sundays at 2 p.m. and 6 p.m. fortnightly. On the Wellington circuit plan of 1824 the entry implied a chapel, but the first chapel actually came into existence in 1829. It faced Station Road beside the *Railway Tavern*, behind the present chapel. It had previously been used as a theatre. The present church was built in 1877, facing Avenue Road.

At the close of the 19th century Methodist meetings took place in the upper part of a disused lime quarry near Limekiln Lane. The quarry, which had been constructed on the 'pillar and stall' method, was sufficient to house a well-attended service. Owing to the danger of subsidence, the plans for building a chapel above ground were abandoned on the advice of an architect from London.

The absence of a specific mention of a church (i.e. a building) in pre-Norman Newport does not infer the absence of one. In Saxon times a building or shed was all that was necessary in country places to cover the portable altar used by the travelling

OPENING

OF THE

New Independent Chapel,

NEWPORT.

On WEDNESDAY, SEPTEMBER the 26th, 1832,

THE REV. J. A. JAMES,

OF BIRMINGHAM,

will Preach in the Afternoon at Half-past Two, and in the Evening at Half-past Six.

ALSO,

On the following SABBATH, SEPTEMBER the 30th,

THE REV. T. WEAVER,

OF SHREWSBURY,

in the Morning at Half-past Ten, and in the Evening at Six o'Clock.

COLLECTIONS will be made after each Service towards defraying the Expenses incurred by the Erection of the said Chapel.

PRINTED BY H. P. SILVESTER.

43. Opening of the New Independent Chapel.

priests, with the congregation standing outside in the open air. Chaucer's Widow of Bath claims to have been married 'at the church door' in her various excursions into matrimony and, indeed, christenings took place there also. Where the numbers warranted it, a nave was built to house the congregation with the rood screen dividing the building. The font moved to the door into the nave and marriages continued at 'the door to the church'.

It is possible that any Saxon building which may have been here would be of little consequence as Newport was only a berewick of Edgmond. After the New Borough was enfranchised the Normans would have replaced any buildings with their own church. Most of the original work in the church has been replaced in three separate restorations in the 19th century.

The Rev. D. H. S. Cranage, writing in 1905, said:

> Newport church is well worth a visit. Most of it has certainly been rebuilt, but the work has been carefully and soundly done, and there are still many ancient features of great architectural and archaeological interest. Reviewing all the evidence, it seems to be fairly established that the tower is late Decorated, with perpendicular signs beginning to appear. The date may be circa 1360, about the same as that of the Nave and Arcade.

As we examine the outside of the building, in the north-west corner of the tower can be seen some slits in the stonework. These are lights to a little room entered from the belfry. It is about eight feet long and is reported to have been the home of a hermit. In a niche on the south side of the tower is a small weather-beaten statue representing Henry I, who gave the town its original charter.

On each side of the west door in the tower there are two newly-carved heads which replaced some badly weatherworn stone. They were carved by Mr. Ervine Shaw of Stafford. One of them is the Prebendary William Budgen, Rector of Newport 1903–22, who in 1912 was responsible for major restoration work on the tower. The dropstone and the arrangement of the plinth suggests the 14th century.

The south porch, a gift of Lady Boughey of Aqualate Hall, was added in 1904 after some houses which had been built close to the church were demolished. By the side of the south porch there is a sculptured crucifix in the modern style, by Mr. Arthur Broadbent, at one time Director of Art at Shrewsbury School.

On entering the church we see the font (bearing the date 1660) which was restored to its present position in 1891 after serving as a flower vase in a gentleman's garden from 1837. From the shape of the 'upper octagonal moulding into round and bottom octagonal' the Reverent Cranage suggests it may be 15th century in date.

The window by the font bears the name of Heane, still familiar through the firm of solicitors in the town. Under the tower, the west window was given by Mr. and Mrs. R. Davies as a contribution to the work of restoration in 1885.

Continuing around the church in a clockwise direction, on the wall over the south porch there is a board bearing the Royal Coat of Arms. After the restoration of Charles II (1660) all churches were required to replace the insignia which had been destroyed by Cromwell's men. An itinerant artist called upon the rector, begging food, and was given the task of painting a new crest.

During the repairs to the roof some interesting carvings were found acting as brackets to the King Posts of the main beams. They are thought to be 'doodlings' of medieval carpenters who were working on the roof. They were removed and mounted on the west wall. Above them is the coat of arms of the Bougheys of Aqualate Hall.

Set in the spandrel of the arch facing the south door is a small medallion of St Andrew. Until 1866 the church was plastered inside, and steep pitched galleries ran around the interior. When these were taken down, and the plaster removed, this figure of St Andrew was discovered, and replaced in the same position when the new pillars were built.

At the west end of the north aisle there is the 'Longford' corner. When St Mary's Church, Longford, was closed, the east window and other movable memorials were transferred to St Nicholas'. Among them is a coat of arms dating from 1808, and the war memorial on which are engraved the names of nine Longford men who gave their lives in the 1914–18 War. This represented about ten per cent of the entire population of the parish. Among the Leeke memorials is one for Colonel Ralph Leeke, who died in 1947. Both his sons having been killed in the First World War, the family thus died out. The small window in the west end of the north aisle, given in memory of the Rev. R. J. Peake, MBS, is the work of Claude Price.

In the west end of the north wall is the window from Longford church, given in memory of the Leeke brothers who were both killed in the 1914–18 War. It is a rare example of the work of Christopher Whall who died in 1924, a very well-known stained glass artist in his day. Some of his major work can be found in Gloucester cathedral. Next to it, opposite the south porch, is a window by Mr. Alan Younger of London. Its theme is 'Creating Infused by the Spirit'.

In the north wall of the north aisle are two segmented pointed arches over a tomb recess.

In 1465, Thomas Reynolds of London, a 'cutteler', in his will 'desired his body to be buried in the Chapel of St Mary in the Collegiate Church of St Nicholas of Newport'. Thomas Reynolds, his son, was resident Canon of the Cathedral Church of Lichfield. The oldest stone in the church built into the wall is probably a tomb fragment. It has a rough cross on it, and may originally have been the lid of a coffin. Could this have been the stone over the grave of Thomas Reynolds?

In 1728, there was extensive restoration work which included the rebuilding of the north and south aisles. 'Unfortunately, aesthetic taste was at a low ebb, and parishioners of that day were more concerned with economy.' (C. C. Barrow).

A few years ago the pews were removed from the north aisle and from the front of the nave and replaced by chairs, which were given by various members of the congregation in memory of a relative or friend. The result is that the north aisle can now be used for meetings and gatherings of various kinds, as well as for exhibitions, and the extra space at the front of the nave allows drama and concerts, both choral and orchestral, to be held in the church which has enabled St Nicholas' to play a much greater part in the cultural life of the community.

The altar in the children's corner at the east end of the north aisle dates from the 18th century. The wrought-iron work was the gift of Thomas Perks, rector from 1722-47, who also left Newport the Perks Charity, from which many young people have benefited.

The sanctuary was furnished by Lady Annabelle Boughey of Aqualate. The reredos is of white Caen stone inlaid with enamel mosaic. On the sides are the figures of St George, St Nicholas, St Andrew, St David, St Chad and St Patrick. The north and south walls are medieval, but the shape of the chancel had been an apse, unusual in a country church of this size, and in the restoration it was rebuilt four-square. The floor is a marble mosaic with two steps of Devonshire marble.

The windows form one of the most interesting collections of modern stained glass in the diocese of Lichfield. The east window over the altar, depicting the Ascension, is by Clayton and Bell, and was a gift in 1891 of the Brittain family. The window in the south wall of the sanctuary is the work of the Pre-Raphaelite artists Edward Burne-Jones and William Morris. The former designed windows, and the latter made them. It was the custom to use the cartoon of a particular figure in more than one window, fitting it into a new design like a piece in a jigsaw puzzle. Both the figures of St John and St Luke have been so used. The two small panels beneath the figures are by Ford Maddox Brown, another distinguished Pre-Raphaelite artist. Other examples of the work of these artists can be found in the windows of the chapel at Jesus College, Cambridge.

On the north wall of the chancel there is a small window over the vestry door. It is glass of a rare quality, Flemish in style. It is a memorial to the first wife of Dr. E. A. Elkington, who was churchwarden at the time of the 'Great Restoration' in 1883-85.

In St Chad's chapel, there are two fine specimens of windows by Kempe, and in each can be found his emblem of a sheaf of corn.

In the east end of the south wall is the Wilbraham window depicting 'the worship of Word and Sacrament'. It is by Mr. Claude Price of Yardley, Birmingham, and in it he uses his method of fusing together, under intense heat, coloured glass, in order to obtain his textures and shades, rather than using the conventional pigment. A letter from him, describing his method of working, hangs beneath the window. The middle window in the south wall was given by members of the Bromfield family in memory of a former churchwarden. The one next to the porch is also by Mr. Claude Price, this time using conventional methods, and not his fused glass technique. A remarkable feature of his work is that he designed, made and fixed his windows entirely on his own, and he had passed his three score years and ten when he undertook these commissions.

Over the arches, set in the north wall, is the Talbot window, depicting Christ and the children of the world against the background of St Nicholas' Church. It was designed and put in by Mr. Joseph Nuttjens. The next window moving east is the Duncan memorial. Originally, there was only the centre light, the two side lights being again the work of Mr. Claude Price. His fused glass technique can be seen in his treatment of the Alpha and Omega symbols. In contrast, the most easterly window in the north wall was designed by a girl in her early twenties, Miss Evelyn Pringle, her first commission for a work of this scale. She was asked to use the words of George Herbert's hymn, and the clear brightness of the glass, with its unusual shapes, is a special feature in her design.

1. Aerial view of Newport, 1983. Preliminary work on the bypass can be seen to the east. The canal can be seen going SW to NE, and marking the limit of the buildings in the south is the site of the disused railway.

2. Sandstone layers in Forton Quarry.

3. Aerial view of an Iron Age fort at Pave Lane.

4. Muster Hill, traditionally the mustering ground for the trained bands and militiamen of the past.

5. The recently restored target butts on Copice Hill once used by the local militia.

7. (*opposite above*) Newport from the church tower, looking north.

8. (*opposite below*) Newport from the church tower, looking south along the High Street.

6. One of the oldest known pictures of Newport, showing the Grammar School, windmill, church and the creamery chimney (demolished 1906). The area shown in the foreground is now a housing estate.

9. Station Road.

10. View of the High Street from Upper Bar.

High St Newport

11. A view taken in the 1930s showing a gas lamp and the war memorial, later removed to Station Road.

12. In the High Street, near the church. The houses on the right were removed to allow widening of the road when the south porch was added to the church.

13. The Square, showing the Wine Vaults.

14. The Butter Cross.

15. The buildings masking the church in this photograph were removed when the south porch was built.

16. The High Street after the removal of the Butter Cross and other buildings.

17. Entering Newport from the north a view of the church is obtained from Lower Bar.

18. The same view today : much the same, only the traffic has changed.

19.   The corner of Wellington Road, showing the rooms of the Literary Institute. The Institute moved to premises in the High Street in 1927.

20.   The road crossing the canal by bridge is so constructed that the bridging effect is not noticed. The houses on the left have now been demolished, and the site is occupied by a filling station.

21. This horse bus was used to convey passengers to and from the railway station which was about half a mile from the town centre.

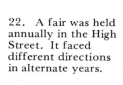

22. A fair was held annually in the High Street. It faced different directions in alternate years.

23. Celebrations to mark Queen Victoria's Jubilee in 1887.

24. Elkes' Dining Rooms, run by the family from 1868.

25. The Canister, a family-run shop, was noted for its cheeses. It was in business from 1920 until 1983.

26. This building was one of the first to be erected after the great fire : it was the *Britannia Inn* and opened in 1667.

27.   Addison's provision shop has been trading since 1885.

28.   Boughey's saddlers shop in the High Street.

29. Scarratt's the outfitters, also in the High Street.

30. Tailors at work in Scarratt's workroom.

31. (*above left*) Mr. and Mrs. Sanders outside the Guildhall, where they ran a hairdressing establishment for many years. Baths were available upstairs at 6d. a time.

32. (*above*) The Millward family outside their bakery shop, which supplied many canal people.

33. (*left*) The alley at Mason's butchery used to lead to the slaughterhouse. The rails for carrying carcases out to the street are still there.

34. (*right*) Cock Alley leads from the High Street to Beaumaris Road.

35. (*below*) This alleyway leads one out of St Mary Street.

36. This was the coach entrance to *The Red Lion*, formerly *The Antelope*, thought to be very near the spot where the great fire began.

37. Various courts or tenements were built on the eastern side of the High Street : this is still called Court No. 3.

38. The lock at Newport.

39. Boats on the Cut.

40. The Skew Bridge.

41. The end of the canal at Wappenshall, where it joins the Trent-Shrewsbury canal. The pool beyond the bridge has been filled up and is now used by a haulage firm. The building has a wharf built underneath it to allow goods to be hauled straight upwards into store.

42. A view along the canal from the bridge showing the basin with the houses of Victoria Park and the swimming pool.

43. Lady Annabelle Boughey whose bequest enabled the Cottage Hospital to be opened in 1930. It is now controlled by the Shropshire Health Authority.

44. The Cottage Hospital.

45. (*above*) Chetwynd House, now converted into flats, has an interesting history. Miss Parker was jilted on her wedding day and from then on lived only in the top floor, keeping her wedding cake in a locked room, until her death aged 84 in 1884. Charles Dickens often stayed at the *Bear Inn* and he may have used this story as a basis for *Great Expectations*.

46. (*left*) Mrs. Millward holding a picture of Miss Parker.

47. A watercolour of Newport Church, done on 1791, showing the apse, later removed.

48. Forton Hall farm and church.

49. Adams' Grammar School and Almshouses.

50. The failure of the windmill to become a profitable enterprise was probably connected with the disappearance of other manufacturing concerns in the town.

51. (*above*) The monument erected on Lilleshall Hill in memory of the Duke of Sutherland.

52. (*right*) Pulestone Cross was erected to the memory of Sir Roger de Pulestone, who was killed fighting the Welsh in the 13th century. The cross is said to have been removed by Parliamentary soldiers during the Civil War.

53. Henry Tudor, claimant to the English throne, landed in Pembrokeshire on 7 August 1485. Sixteen days later he won the crown with a victory at the battle of Bosworth. In 1985 the march was commemorated and the party halted at Newport, one of Henry's original camps 500 years before. Here the force is seen entering the town.

54. This plaque on a house in Vauxhall Terrace, Salter's Lane commemorates one of the first government rehousing schemes. The occupants were moved here from the Marsh Estate.

An alabaster tomb in the chapel, with the statues of a man and woman, is that of Judge Salter and his wife. It dates from 1492. A more recent addition is the reredos in St Chad's chapel, given by past and present members of the Girls' Friendly Society. Incorporating local scenes into medieval religious paintings was common practice in the Middle Ages and, although much artistic licence has been used, it portrays the Nativity in the setting of Newport, with the trees at Forton in the background. The artist was Denise Bates.

On the south wall of the chapel is an icon donated by the Serbian Orthodox Church, Donnington. When Longford Church was closed, its bell was given to the Serbian Church.

The church bells have featured not infrequently in the parish registers:

1662   '. . . that ye bels of Newport new made to the gallery this month'
1662   'this month we ye loft built for ringing or a belfree'
1701   '. . . that on ye 9th of April last, one John Bellringer being accidentally killd by ye 2d Bell, ye said bell became forfeited to ye Earle of Bradford; but upon ye parishioners acknowledgement, his Lordship as freely returned ye Bell being thus forfeited as his Grandfather at first gave it when it was founded, and in acknowledgement of ye favour we have hereunto set our names.

Jn. Greenwood Minr   2 churchwardens

2 overseers   2 constables   13 other names

The forfeiture was under the ancient law of *Deodand*, whereby anything animate or inanimate, causing the death of a person, became the property of the Lord of the Manor, to do with as he wished. This law was repealed in 1846.

By 1871, the population of the town had risen over the three thousand mark, a rise of 1,000 from 1801. The number of commercial establishments listed, both industrial and retail, had risen to 180. This increase had given more responsibilities to the commonalty who, by election, had more control of the affairs of the town.

An Act of George III (1764) had stated that the Town Hall and Butter Cross, given to the town in Adams' will (1660), were the property of the Marsh Trustees. This was repealed by the Newport (Salop) Marsh Improvement Act, 1854, and the property was vested in a trust for improving the town — without affecting the rights of the lords of the manor, who still drew 20s. as chief rent. This Act allowed the trustees to demolish the Town Hall and Butter Cross and to make the sites a portion of the High Street, rebuilding the town hall elsewhere. The Newport (Salop) Market Company Incorporated Act of 1858 empowered the corporation to 'build a Market House and Market Place and other buildings for Public Accommodation, and establish and regulate Markets and fairs there, opening a new street and widening other streets'. The corporation proposed to accommodate the Marsh Trustees in order to obviate the necessity of the trustees rebuilding the town hall. The new market hall, corn exchange, assembly room and Smithfield were completed in 1860, the various rooms in the hall being used by different organisations.

The preamble of the 1858 Newport, Salop, Markets Act is very explicit:

Whereas markets and fairs have for many years been held in the town of Newport in the County of Salop, for the sale of Horses, cattle, sheep, pigs, meat, poultry, fish, vegetables and other commodities, and whereas the said markets and fairs are now held, partly in the streets and partly in the town hall and in a building called the Butter Cross, to the great obstruction of the thoroughfare and to the danger and inconvenience of passengers through the same, and it would be advantageous to the inhabitants of the said town and of the neighbourhood thereof if the same were abolished, and if a commodious and sufficient Market House and market place and rooms to be used or let for the transaction of public and other business within the said town with suitable buildings and accommodation connected therewith and approaches thereto were provided. And whereas it would also be for the public advantage if power were given to the Company to be incorporated by this Act to acquire by purchase or by lease, or otherwise, all the market and fair tolls, dues, stallages, standings, and payments now leviable and demandable within the said town and to establish and regulate proper markets, and if the tolls, rents, rates, dues, stallages and charges to be taken is such markets and fairs and for the same use of such market places, market houses, rooms and other conveniences therein respectively were defined etc.

In the 26th section of the Act it was noted that 'the tolls and other dues now payable in the said markets and fairs held within the said town of Newport, are now vested in the Most Noble George Granville, Duke and Earl of Sutherland, his heirs and assigns'.

In a national reorganisation of chartered towns in 1883, Newport was listed among those places which after the operation of the Act would cease to be boroughs, unless a new charter were granted by Queen Victoria. Newport did not seek a new charter of Incorporation and, in accordance with the provisions of the Act, the local government board (originally the Sanitary Board) was vested with the properties, liberties, franchises etc., of the former corporation.

The Municipal Corporations (Unreformed) Bill made provisions for such corporations and in 1886 the corporation of the borough was dissolved, and the district of the local board of Newport came into being on the 25th March 1886 with the following provisos:

1. All property vested in the Corporation to be vested in the local board;
2. All property real and personal, except Symonds Charity and property held as trustees of any charity vested in the board;
3. The Public Health Act, 1875, to apply;
4. Property vested in the local board by paragraph 2 has been used by the Corporation for water undertaking and it is expedient that the property and income should continue to be applied for the water supply of the district;
5. Local board to keep a separate account for water supply;
6. All liabilities of the Corporation enforceable against the local board.

The local board began acquiring and reorganising the various services. They had already, of course, the management of the water supply.

In 1878 the Newport Gas, Light and Coke Company Ltd. (founded in 1835) was ordered 'to supply 67 lamp posts, lamps and lamp lighters and everything else necessary and proper for lighting the public lamps, except during the moonlight nights when it shall be at the discretion of the manager, so as not to inconvenience the public'.

Cleaning the streets and the removal of house refuse were also provided for:

1. To remove and carry away to a depot provided by himself and approved by the council, all road scrapings and sweepings once in every day from the High Street and St Mary Street

with the Wellington Road, and carry away all scrapings when dry, accumulating in all other roads throughout the U.D.C.

2. On Saturday mornings each week by 9.30 a.m. remove without spilling all ashes and other like refuse deposited by the inhabitants along the High Street and St Mary Street between the canal bridge and Wellington Road.

3. Once in 4 weeks, clean and carry away, without making any avoidable nuisance, the contents of all cess pools in the U.D. and clean away any contents that may be shed in cleansing.

4. As the surveyor deems necessary will water by cart the whole of the main streets from the *Bridge Tavern* at Chetwynd End to the approach of the Railway station and Stafford Street, to the 'Old Toll Gate' and to the Mill in the Forton Road.

In 1879 the expenses in the financial statement of the Newport (Salop) local government board district were only those of the gas supply and 'scavenging and watering'. By 1894 when the constituted Newport (Salop) Urban District Council was in full control, the expense sheet included the gas company, scavenging, sanitary work, manual labour, materials, team work on roads, tradesmen's bills, street works and improvements, hospital, fire engine, and salaries.

44. Steam locomotive.

VIII

NEWPORT, SHROPSHIRE

By the end of the 19th century, Newport was the seat of local government for the surrounding area. His Grace the Duke of Sutherland was lord of the manor, and held court leets annually. The county court, established under the County Court Act of 1864, sat once a month in the Town Hall for the recovery of debts to any amount not exceeding £20. By the close of the century, the county court was sitting every two months with a judge and jury and also dealt with cases of bankruptcy.

The growth of the population over the 150 years from 1800 is very steady in comparison with the increase in the number of small industries. The first 50 years from 1801 show an increase of ten per cent. per year in the number of small businesses. During the following 50 years, however, when the population remained steady, the small industries died out, and a single larger one took their place.

Writing the history of Newport, one sometimes feels that it is no more than a chronicle of things which have disappeared. The town hall, with what was reputed to be the best dance floor in Shropshire, is not now used for that purpose. Before 1916, a committee of 20 members ran a weekly dance in the lower room, each winter from November until Lent. At Christmas they held a children's party. Once a month there was a ball upstairs (30s. entry, including refreshments.) (See advert. facing page.)

In the part of the hall once used as a corn exchange, a cinema once operated, run by the Wright brothers who started it with a projector in lieu of a bad debt in 1913. In the silent days the piano accompanist was Mr. Foxhall, with Mr. Dodd from the *Bridge Inn* on the violin. Mr. Dodd also produced the roar of the MGM lion on his 'cello. The first sound was on records with the picture. The first real talkie shown in the cinema was the black and white *Broadway Melody*. Once, being short of film for a children's matinee, they were offered a new film to try out. It was to become famous as *Batman*. The Wrights made their own sound equipment to match the perfect acoustics of the hall. Each year at pantomime time, the cinema was closed for two weeks while a professional touring company took it over. Changes in the way of life caused the cinema to close down and the space is now used as a covered market. Films are now shown in the renovated Cosy Hall in Water Lane.

The best days of the cattle market are now gone. In the early part of the century, cattle and sheep used to arrive and depart by railway, being driven up the High Street, until the days of the cattle trucks bringing them from the farm direct to the market.

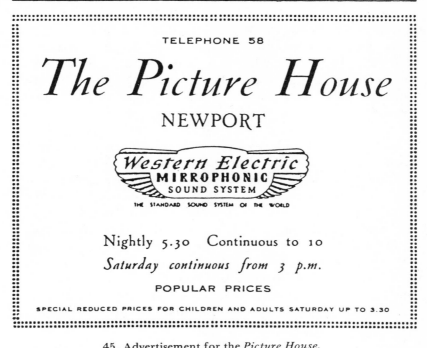

148 "Newport & Market Drayton Advertiser" Almanack, Diary and Directory

TELEPHONE 58

The Picture House

NEWPORT

Western Electric
MIRROPHONIC
SOUND SYSTEM

THE STANDARD SOUND SYSTEM OF THE WORLD

Nightly 5.30 Continuous to 10

Saturday continuous from 3 p.m.

POPULAR PRICES

SPECIAL REDUCED PRICES FOR CHILDREN AND ADULTS SATURDAY UP TO 3.30

45. Advertisement for the *Picture House*.

The busy market days when the farmers and their wives brought their butter, eggs and dressed fowls are gone. The cattle market is now held on Mondays, with an open domestic market on Fridays and Saturdays.

The slaughterhouse behind Mason's butcher shop is closed, although the overhead rails which were used to bring the carcasses to the High Street can still be seen in the passageway. A steam flour mill was in operation next to it in the early part of the century. This was operated by Mr. Pascall, a noted gingerbread maker.

The rope walk, which was parallel with the Smithfield, has closed down, and the local hemp butts have disappeared.

The tannery situated at the corner of Stafford Street and Water Lane was taken over by Talbots, the local builders. In 1791 a fire had destroyed it, '59 tons of bark being consumed'. It was rebuilt and, as late as 1908, was producing '30 tons of leather a year from 2,000 hides for boots and shoes'. When it closed down, the stream which ran past it was piped under the canal into the Strine. The Slinn family in Upper Bar were making boots and shoes for the gentry in the surrounding estates, and the inhabitants of Newport from 1860 until 1941.

The Elkes family started a bakery in Middle Row in 1868 and by 1900 had established a Temperance Hotel, where commercial travellers coming to the area by railway could stay, while they travelled around the country by pony and trap to conduct their business. They also had a restaurant, which was kept very busy on market days. Another branch of the family set up a biscuit factory in Uttoxeter and, exactly 100 years after they came to Newport, the business in the town finished and the premises were taken over by the Midland Bank.

Next door to them, Dawsons, which had connections by marriage with the Elkes family, carried on a basket-making business. The osiers were grown on the side of the canal west of the bridge and dried in a shed near Polly's Lock. There they were dried and peeled and brought into the cellar of the shop where they were woven into baskets to suit the customers. One of their specialities was wicker baskets for venison and game birds shot on the big estates, which were transported to London by the railway. Bigger tradesmen's hampers were made to order; the Elkes' three-wheeled bread baskets were also made by them. The Dawsons also had a carriage business in Station Road, making light traps and landaus. The site is now occupied by a garage.

From 1804 until 1948, the Brittain family, grocers, tea dealers, seed merchants and tallow chandlers had their business in the High Street. Their curtilage ran down to Audley Road, with the building where they melted the fat, which they bought from the butchers, to make tallow candles for the miners at Ketley and the general populace. They did an extensive trade with the local gentry, selling various specialities like bottled cocks' combs and bottled *champignons* (French mushrooms). American belly bacon in brine arrived by canal in strong wooden boxes, which were themselves sold as a profitable sideline. The firm was one of the first to make their own electricity with a generator.

In 1887 Richard Brittain of Summerhill and Edwin Whittingham, builder, 'now agreed to sell for £100 to the trustees to make a road 36 ft. wide as a means of connection between the estate vested in the trustees and the Station Road in Newport to continue to form a junction with Audley Avenue to be finished by 31 December 1888. To plant plane trees at 40 ft. distances on either side of the said road and will properly stake and renew the same as and when may be necessary until the said road shall become the responsibility of the inhabitants at large'. This road became Granville Avenue.

The demand for milk in the big towns allowed some farmers to send their milk to Birmingham by railway, but the United Dairies had a mill and a creamery in Forton Road. After it was closed down, the buildings were used for intensive egg production during the 1914–18 War. The chimney was demolished in 1930 and the site is now a garage.

In the early part of the 19th century, the demand from mill-owners for a safer form of lighting than the whale oil and Russian tallow lamps led to the use of gas which was produced in the manufacture of coke. The only practical method was to provide gas mains from the generator. In 1835 a company was formed in Newport to use this idea and an oven and two gasometers holding 8,000 cubic feet each were set up in Avenue Road. This method was used to light the town until the industry was nationalised and eventually the plant was closed down, leaving one gasometer, fed from Wellington, to act as a reservoir and pressure regulator. The system is now on the North Sea gas supply and the gasometer is due for dismantling.

Although the site of 'Ashworth's' is now a building estate and the sound of their time siren is heard no more, they were for 35 years one of the main industries in the town. John Ashworth & Co. (Timber) Ltd. had specialised in the conversion of home grown timber since 1856. They first opened a branch in Newport at Pave Lane in 1924 buying the saw mill and yard in Station Road the following year. The company was one of the first to realise the potential of kiln drying timber and early in the 1930s, they installed a battery of kilns at their Newport premises. One of their specialities was the production of high grade English oak for interior decorative work, and among the many projects that they were connected with was the supply of the English oak used for the rebuilding of the House of Commons after the 1939–45 War.

The 'railway mania' nearly turned Newport into a mini Crewe junction. At various times, the following proposals were put forward:

1844	Grand Junction Railway from near Stafford through Wellington to Shrewsbury.
1845	Stafford and Shropshire Junction Railway through Wellington to Shrewsbury. This plan involved the conversion of the Newport branch of the Shropshire Union Canal into a railway, using the actual canal bed where practicable.
1845	Shropshire Mineral Railway, from Stafford through Norbury, Newport, Lilleshall to Much Wenlock.
1861	Market Drayton and Newport Junction Railway.
1862	Shifnal, Newport, Norton Bridge.
1898	Light Railway between Donnington and Hinstock via Lilleshall and Newport to Cheswardine.
1922	Newport and Four Ashes Light Railway via Wheaton Aston and Brewood.

One thing the railway did was to make travel very much faster and break down the isolation in rural areas caused by earlier difficulties in communication. Apart from the benefit of easier personal travel in and out of the town, the railway helped local agriculture by enabling milk and other perishable goods to reach a wider market. The large towns, where horses were still used for local transport, needed a good supply of fodder. Another side-effect of the railway was the increasing improvement in the feeder roads to the stations.

The absence of large-scale industry in the town and the coming of private cars and motorised transport minimised the railway's effectiveness in the area in 1968, under the Beeching Plan, the line was closed down. In the *Newport and Market Drayton Advertiser*, 27 September 1968, a sad note was struck:

> When British Rail's diesel engine number 8J02 chugged out of Newport Station's yard on Monday, it was making a small place for itself in the annals of local history.

It was indeed an historic day, marking the end of 199 years' connection of the railway with Newport. Originally, the station was about half a mile from the town and, although houses were built along the approaches to it, the main building programme in the town was well away from the station. An omnibus used to collect and convey the passengers to and from the main inns and any other part of the town. It was horse-drawn of course, the forerunner of the taxi service outside stations today.

It is always interesting to study the road systems of a town and wonder whether or not the settlement originated because of the roads or the roads gained importance by passing through the town. In Newport we have examples of both ideas. At first glance today, Newport is a 'crossroads' town and gains its importance from this fact. The road systems radiating from Newport and the evidence of the 1950 traffic census would infer that it has grown as a junction of main routes. But we know that one of the reasons for its origin was the road we now call the A41, so it would be more correct to say that the other routes derived from the presence of the town on this road.

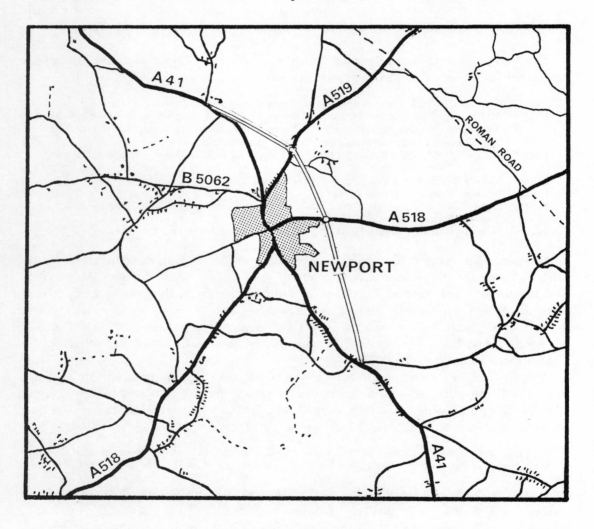

| ▬▬▬▬ 'A' roads | ━━━━Other roads | ░░░ Settlements | ═══ Bypass |

(from O.S. 1 inch sheet 119)

46. The main routes through Newport.

The B5062, in Norman times the link between the demesne manor at Edgmond and the seat of the Earl of Shrewsbury, never had the importance of a trade route, and although now well used by the Milk Marketing Board at Crudgington Dairy and the Shrewsbury Cattle Market, is still only ranked as a 'B' road. Originally, Salter's Lane continued past Longford Hall to Donnington and Wellington, but this fell into disuse.

The limestone industry at Lilleshall emphasised the importance of the Wellington Road (A518). It now leads to the A5 and North Wales, and branching from the A5 at Shrewsbury, by the A458, to mid-Wales. The Severn Valley via Dawley and South Wales via Shrewsbury are also reached by the Wellington Road exit from Newport.

The A519 through Forton may have been, in early times, a road from the Cheshire salt producing areas but, as industry developed in the 19th century, it was a link between the Potteries and the Coalbrookdale and Ironbridge area. With the Stafford Road (A518), it became important enough to be turnpiked.

As Birmingham expanded in the 19th century and sought an export trade through the Mersey ports, the A41 became of vital importance, and it is now ranked as a trunk road. The early Roman Road from Gailey to Hinstock via Wilbrighton had disappeared. When the centre of the lock-making industry had moved from Brewood to Wolverhampton, the Birmingham–Wolverhampton–Newport stretch became the most important part of the road. Telford's A5 to Holyhead diverted the flow for a time, only to be replaced by increased volume to the Mersey ports.

It has been estimated that in the early 19th century as many as 2,000 horses were associated with Newport. In view of the traffic passing through the town, the number of cars parked on the streets and in garages, what would be the equivalent in horse power today? The stabling for horses has given place to car parks and the feeding to petrol stations, the harness makers to garage mechanics.

Trying to do a traffic census with a difference, we noted the addresses of the lorries passing through the town for half an hour on three separate days. Leaving out the various towns in the Birmingham conurbation and local lorries, we can see from the map (page 90), the widespread area which uses Newport as a throughway.

The railways had made their mark on the carriage business and, with their speedier transport, caused the eventual drift of trade away from the canals, but a new invention, the internal combustion engine, brought the roads back into prominence as a means of communication throughout the country. The production of Henry Ford's Model 'T' supplied the first cheap motor car, and in 1904 the compulsory registration of cars was introduced in England with a maximum speed of 20 m.p.h. The first car registered in Shropshire — AW 1 — was owned by Captain Foster of Woodcote Hall, President at that time of the Newport Literary Institute.

The first bus in Newport — a charabanc — appeared just after the First World War, run by Mr. Beard, when he retired it was sold to Austin's at Woodseaves, the beginning of the Happy Days buses. W. Wheat, builders' merchant, the forerunner of Wheat & Kirby still operating in the town, used a steam lorry for his heavy deliveries.

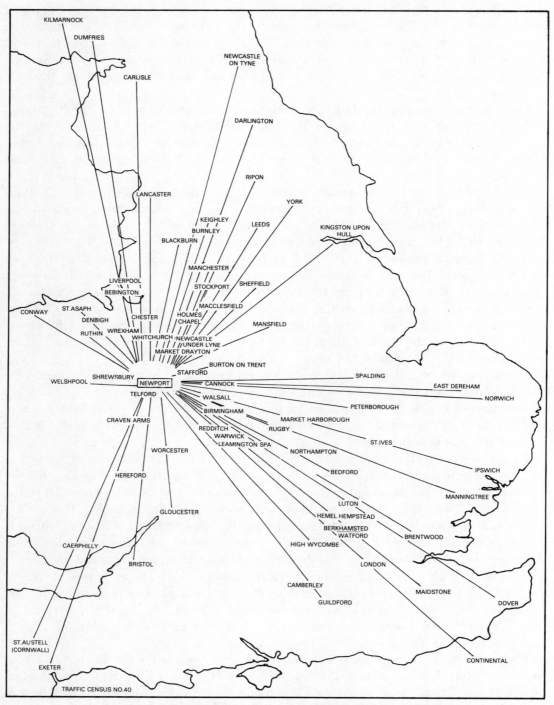

47. Points of origin of lorries passing through Newport.

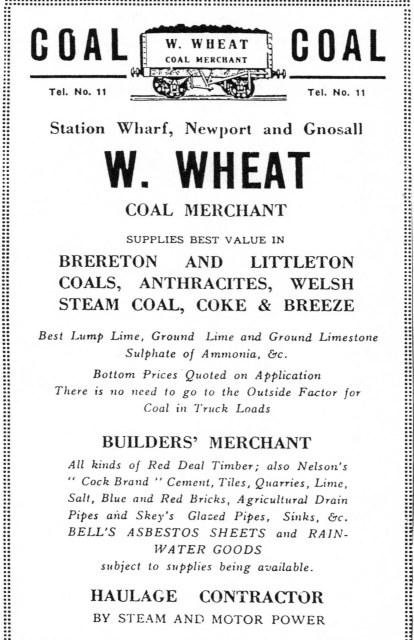

48. Advertisement for W. Wheat, coal merchant.

VELOCIPEDES AND EXCURSIONISTS

To the Editor of the NEWPORT ADVERTISER.

SIR,—There is no foretelling to what extent the utility of the canoe on the water, and the velocipede on the land, may be carried in aiding the active excursionist in visiting different parts of the country and in penetrating into the pleasant invigorating nooks and corners of the land. To the lover of nature and beautiful scenery they are, in my opinion, likely to become a common boon, especially to the working classes, for they may be able to travel by them when and where they like, and to loiter at any snug roadside inn or pleasant locality their fancy may dictate. They will, by the use of the velocipede, be able to avoid the crowd, bustle, and danger of "the line", and the inconvenience of railway time, and also the expense of travelling thereby. Now as one person can easily travel from 70 to 100 miles per day, I see no reason why there should not be an improvement made so as to carry four or six or even more persons with their necessary baggage, with their increased propelling powers at the same or greater speed for any reasonable length of time they may require, and be the means of bringing occasional visitors to those neglected towns which have never had as yet a fair opportunity of reaping a small share of the benefit received from railway travellers and excursionists, who are whirled to distant dull seaports, and the largest towns in the kingdom, selected by the railway companies themselves; leaving many of our pleasant and inviting inland towns and lovely villages unheeded, unnamed, and unknown—which to the inhabitants of huge and pent up towns and cities would prove a very agreeable exchange where "touters" are unknown and imposition less probable.

The velocipede at no very distant day may give an impetus to the local trade here, for your enterprising townsman, Mr. William Underhill, is extending his manufacture considerably, and his trade in general seems on the increase, if we may judge from the nature of the large building and ironfoundry now erecting near the Newport Gas Works.

The bi-cycle, which is the marvel of the million as to the difficulty of preserving its balance, can never become so useful or general as the velocipede; but the difficulty of using it will be at once dispelled by visiting any of the practicing rooms, of which there are eight or nine now in London, which one may see crowded with staid city merchants, stockbrokers, and West End exquisites receiving instructions, or whirling round the area as vivid as thought. You will find them describing their easy and rapid locomotion as an enjoyment positively intense. Itching to share in it, bashfulness will soon disappear, under the persuasion of the riding master and those who,

"Swearing ne'er to consent, consented",

when, after a few visits, it is ten to one that you go to Mr. Davis, 14, Strand, London (the agent of the French Velocipede Company), or nearer home to Mr. W. Underhill, Newport, Salop, and get supplied with a velocipede for home use. It will be a cheap doctor, and enjoyed throughout the year; can be had by men of little means; saves time, and is likely ultimately to become the people's iron pleasure-horse—requiring neither farrier, groom, nor corn.

Yours, very respectfully,

Pilson, 19th May, 1869.   J.W.

49. Letter to the *Newport Advertiser* on cycling, 1869.

In the Lower Bar, Belle Vue cycles were manufactured in conjunction with a Ford agency carried on in premises eventually taken over by Hogben's garage in 1934. The nurses' home, now the grammar school buildings, was supplied with electricity from their generator.

A water supply is needed not only for domestic or business use, but also for fighting fires. There was no municipal service for dealing with this problem until the insurance companies in the early 19th century campaigned for the provision of fire engines. An Act of 1843 allowed parishes to provide engines and pipes at a charge on the rates. Newport spent £50 on a fire engine which was kept in the part of the church which had been the previous chantry, with the vestry built over it. This was a manual pump drawn by whatever horses could be commandeered. After the church restoration, the pump was housed in the town hall and later in the council yard in Salter's Lane. When a fire was reported, a man was detailed to open the valves to give the volume of water needed in the hydrants, and to close them after the emergency to keep the supply constant to domestic users. Later, a pulsometer trailer pump was bought, but a vehicle had to be commandeered to transport it. The modern fire service with proper equipment and personnel was first installed in its own headquarters in Salter's Lane in 1957.

The first mention of a policeman in Newport was when 'the son of a policeman' was accepted into the Grammar School in 1838. Under the Municipal Corporation Act (1835) Watch Committees had been set up in boroughs to appoint constables. Newport already had its patrol both day and night, quartered in the Booth Hall. By 1856 a 'lock up' had been built in Stafford Road which by 1900 was staffed by an Inspector and five constables but, by 1926, this force was reduced to a sergeant and two constables. A new police station was opened in Wellington Road in 1950.

The High School for Girls was founded by the county in 1919, taking over the local scholars from Merivale College. The present premises were first occupied in 1925 with a staff of ten teachers. There was a preparatory department until 1944, when the school was designated for secondary education alone. During the war, the school housed a school from Smethwick.

Castle House Private Preparatory School was opened in 1944 in part of the buildings which had housed Merivale College. The pupils are taken up to entry to secondary education. The name Castle House derives from a wall built around the garden, in the manner of a castle. Another feature of the building is the many different fossils cemented into the walls.

Burton Borough School was founded as a secondary modern school in 1957, Colonel J. G. Burton Borough being chairman of the governors. The name of the school was changed to Burton Borough in 1973. The number on the original roll was 349, but considerable expansion has resulted in a roll of 870 in 1984. Additions to the buildings have been rooms for art, craft, wood and metal working, and technical drawing. French and geology have also been added to the curriculum. A minibus, supplied by the active parent-teachers' association in 1968, is fully used in educational visits and for sports teams. Both the archery and cycling teams have gained success at national level.

Adams Grammar School entered the century with an increase in resident boarders and became fully secondary in 1944 with German and French in the curriculum as well as physics, chemistry and biology. Many of the pupils go on to university. As an Honorary Freeman of the Worshipful Company of Haberdashers, the founder governors of the school, Her Royal Highness, Princess Margaret, visited the school in 1968. There are now three infant schools and two junior schools in the town.

The population increase from 1901 to 1961 parallels the establishment of the Audley Engineering Company in the town, but the catchment area of their workforce covered quite a few of the surrounding villages. To balance this, many of the towns-people were travelling out to work in Stafford, Donnington or Wellington.

THE GROWTH IN POPULATION

1801 — 2,307	1901 — 3,241	1951 — 3,744	1961 — 4,369
1965 — 5,260	1971 — 7,020	1975 — 7,370	1981 — 9,053

In 1972, Newport Urban District Council was forced, by an Act of Parliament, to merge with other councils. The decision to join the Wrekin District Council in 1974 was taken voluntarily, provided that Newport retained its status as a town with town council and a mayor.

The various areas of responsibility today are outlined below:

COUNTY COUNCIL

Education
Library
Police (West Mercia)
Fire services
Roads, pavements, footpaths
Road cleansing
Road drainage
Main road lighting
Transport policy
Audley House
Grants
Refuse disposal
Parking restrictions
School managers and
    governors
Social services
Road safety
Trading standards

WREKIN COUNCIL

Refuse collection
Skip site
Street cleansing
Public conveniences
Pollution control
Food inspection
Planning controls
Building regulations
Improvement grants
Housing
Sewers (Severn Trent Agents)
Swimming pool
Sports/play areas
Canal/open spaces
Play leadership
Grants
Street collections
Home safety
Car parks
Taxis (Licensing)
Rates/rate rebates
Rent rebates

TOWN COUNCIL

Cemetery
Churchyard
Swimming pool trust
Planning (observations)
Grants
Accident prevention
Social car scheme
Home defence
Footway lighting
Representatives on Charitable
    Trusts
Bus shelters
'Watchdog' for all
    town facilities

INLAND REVENUE

House rating assessments

SEVERN TRENT WATER AUTHORITY

Water supply
Sewage disposal

MINISTRY OF TRANSPORT

A 41 (County as agents). The new bypass
    becomes the A 41, the present A 41 through
    the town will lose trunk road status.

SHROPSHIRE AREA HEALTH AUTHORITY

Ambulance service
Clinic (Beaumaris Road)
Cottage hospital
Doctors
Dentists
Opticians
NB: Community Health Council
    League of Friends

POST MASTER

Post Office facilities,
    including post boxes,
    public telephones

MIDLAND ELECTRICITY BOARD

Maintenance of street lights

Other bodies with special responsibilities include the Civic Society, the Gas Council, the Electricity Council, the Post Office Users Council, and the Citizens' Advice Bureau (at Wellington).

The town's appearance today demonstrates Newport to be a settlement which has maintained a relatively unchanged status over the centuries where other towns have experienced expansion and decay. In 1961, the town was still centred around the High Street with small courts behind the shops and also some houses on the Audley or Marsh estates.

A plaque in Vauxhall Terrace commemorates one of the first council rehousing schemes in the country. The stone was laid on 11 May 1927 by W. Wheat, J.P., Chairman of the Council and A. E. Evans, Chairman of the Housing Committee. The first experiment in housing the overspill from Birmingham in 1967 led to the construction of owner-occupied houses which have multiplied until the population has been doubled in 20 years. Many of the working adults now travel to neighbouring towns so that Newport is now facing the situation of adapting to the role of a dormitory town, while still retaining the atmosphere of a market town.

One of Telford's most difficult projects, the canal, has been in disuse for several years and the cost of renovating so many locks prohibited the use of the waterway purely for pleasure craft. The stables on the wharf and warehouses are gone, but the stretch through the town has been kept filled and landscaped. It is now a pleasant walk and a fishery.

The busy foundry on the canal side has closed and the buildings have been taken down; a garage occupies the site.

The increase in wartime of wheat production which had been harvested by combine harvesters, and could not be stored in corn stacks to dry out before threshing, meant that a new form of storing had been found. A chain of 16 government silos was built, one of them in Avenue Road in Newport, next to the Audco factory. Twenty bins, 125 feet high, were built to hold 5,000 tons of grain. The capacity has been increased to 6,000 tons and barley as well as wheat is now stored. Diesel fuel air heaters have now replaced the original steam powered heaters. A thriving small industrial estate has grown up near the silo.

Once again, Newport has a foundry in operation and a milk bottling dairy has been established together with a construction firm and garden furniture suppliers.

The main industry in the town is Serck Audco Valves, which was originally established in 1896. The company took over the premises of Mr. Underhill, who manufactured and repaired agricultural machinery on a site which he had purchased from the Marsh Trustees. The Audley Engineering Company was registered as a limited company in 1906 making iron cock and other valves, but by the 1920s cock valves up to three inches in size were being produced. A licence to manufacture a pressurised lubricant gland cock enabled the firm to produce, during the last war, valves for the 'Pluto' submarine pipeline and 'Fido' installations for the dispersal of fog on the airfields.

For those of us who knew English market towns when agriculture played a central part in the atmosphere of the community (the market days with the sheep and the cattle going to and from the railway station and the market, the weekly shopping days with the pubs open all day) it is easy to say that the last war changed everything. It is also easy to say that the influx of multiple stores and the advent of new housing estates have changed the town. But, looking back through the centuries, we see that this is only another opportunity for the town to react to new circumstances. Taking a broad view it would seem that the town is back to the days, 200 years ago, when roads were the normal means of travel. On 19th October 1984 the new bypass was opened taking the heavy lorries and some of the holiday traffic away from the High Street. The challenge now, is how will the town react to this third road across the valley?

Newport was founded as a market town. Throughout its life it has remained thus. Whatever the pressures, both within and without, it has remained faithful to this role. It has disregarded industrialisation and is still a town of traders.

50. A Model 'T' Ford motor-car.

APPENDIX I

SOME LOCAL STATELY HOMES

AQUALATE HALL

Before the Conquest the park was in the manor of Meretown. In 1204 King John gave it to the Archbishop of Canterbury to found a monastery. In 1435 there was a fortified manor at Mereton, owned by the Butler family, who sold it for £400 to Thomas Skrymsher of Norbury Manor in 1515. He built the first important house on the site of the present one.

Forton Hall was built in 1665; Wren rebuilt the east end of the present house and called it Aqualate Hall. The estate was bought in 1795 by Sir Thomas Fletcher, an industrialist, partly financed by the Bougheys who were descended in the female line from Sir Robert de Booth, killed at the battle of Blore Heath.

In 1805, Sir John Fenton Boughey was Lord of the Manor. His son Thomas married Lady Annabelle. Sir Thomas, as Chairman of the U.D.C., was the driving force in the reorganisation of the water supply and new sewage schemes. He was also President of the Literary Institute, and one of the founders of the Newport & District Agricultural Society.

LONGFORD HALL

Longford was an important manor at the time of Domesday, being held by two knights in return for military service. By 1274, Adam de Brimpton held it for one knight's fee, i.e. 'he was bound at his own cost to provide a guard, with a barbed horse, for forty days whenever the King approached Wales'. This was required of him in 1277; his son was summoned to serve against the Scots in 1301.

In 1556, a John Talbot, son of the sixth earl of Shrewsbury, married Margaret Troutbeck who inherited one-third of the manors of Edgmond and Newport. Longford was their residence and their grandson John became earl of Shrewsbury in 1630 on the death of his uncle. The Talbots were staunch Roman Catholics and Royalists.

In 1788, Longford Hall passed into the hands of the Leeke family, who were involved in the affairs of the town until the death of Colonel Ralph Leeke.

The estate has been acquired by Adams Grammar School, the house being used as a dormitory for the boarders.

LILLESHALL HALL

At one time the residence of the Duke of Sutherland, now Lilleshall Hall National Sports Centre. A great many pre-1914 house-sale catalogues have been placed on permanent loan to the History Society by Mr. E. N. Podmore, a member of a local farming family. They provide an extensive picture of the agriculture of the area, and include the 1917 sale catalogue of the Sutherland Estates, which covered nearly 19,000 acres in the late 1800s.

CHETWYND

Newport Salop.   Chetwynd Park

In Domesday Book Turold de Verley was said to hold both Longford and Chetwynd. The Countess Godiva held Chetwynd (in Edward's time) when it was worth 25s. 'Now', says the record, 'it is worth 50s.'. The manor later passed to a wealthy family who took the name Chetwynd.

In 1318 Reginald de Chetwynd became interested in making money from the many cattle coming out of Wales, to offset the shortage in England due to famine. He approached the King to set up a market to rival Newport which was beginning to develop into a town of importance.

The Pigot family bought the estate at the end of the 15th century and were in residence until 1774. In 1803 Thomas Borough became owner of the Hall; his heir John Charles Burton Borough served as Sheriff of Shropshire in 1844. The family had a long association with the town, commemorated in the title of the Burton Borough School.

GLOSSARY

Alienation: The transfer of a holding by sale rather than by inheritance. A lord could not alienate his estate without a licence from the Crown.

Artesian Well: One with enough pressure for the water to reach the surface.

Berewick: A subsidiary or outlying estate.

Booth Hall: A hall for displaying and selling goods.

Bordars: A cottager. Usually engaged in menial work.

Boor: A free peasant, above a serf but below a thane. Usually associated with milk cattle.

Burgage: A piece of land, usually less than half an acre held in a borough of the Crown or lords of the borough.

Cooper: A maker or repairer of barrels.

in Capite: Tenant in chief who held his land immediately of the Crown.

Carbon-dating: Measurement of the radioactive carbon in organic materials.

Clay: A very finely powdered soil containing hydrated aluminium silicate. Is plastic when moist but hardens when heated.

Demesne: Land of the manor held in the lord's own hands. The villein tenants had an obligation to work on the demesne lands.

Dunes: A mound or ridge of drifted loose sand.

Danegeld: A tax raised in the 10th century to give as a tribute to the Danes to prevent them invading England.

Era: A major division of geological time divided into several periods.

Erratic: A piece of rock which differs in composition from the rock surrounding it having been transported from its place of origin.

Esker: A long winding ridge of gravel etc., deposited by a meltwater stream running under a glacier.

Forest: Applied to a piece of land kept for hunting by the King. Verderers were responsible for their preservation.

Frank Pledge: A system whereby members of a tithing (10 men) were responsible for each others' behaviour; view of Frank Pledge, inspection by authorities to ensure it existed.

Furlong: Originally, a furrow length in the open fields eventually standardised as one-eighth of a mile, i.e., 10 chains. One chain wide by ten chains long is equal to an acre.

Guild: A trade guild restricted its numbers and imposed rules as to apprenticeship, quality of goods handled, etc.

Geld: Originally Saxon term for money. A tribute in terms of gold.

Glacial Lake: A temporary lake formed by enclosing the meltwater inside higher land.

Hide: Originally the amount of land which could be ploughed in a year and support a family. Varied in size with the quality of the land etc.

Hundred: A division of a shire for government purposes. Influence of hundred court gave way to parochial and manor courts and the Justices of the Peace.

Indenture: Originally, a document cut through the middle or written twice with the word indenture cut through to prove the authenticity of each part.

Inquisition: An inquiry into the possessions of a person holding them from the Crown and assessing the heir to them.

Ley Line: A line joining two prominent points in the landscape thought to be the line of a pre-historic track.

Manor: A landed estate.

Meanders: A river following a winding course. Usually in flat country.

Meltwater: Melted snow or ice.

Mere: A shallow lake or marsh.

Mewed: Sparrow hawk — a one year old.

Moulding Sand: Sand suitable for making a mould for casting metals.

Neat Herd: A cowherd appointed by the community to prevent cattle straying.

Norbroom: Common grazing land of the settlement.

Passage: Toll for the passage of goods or passengers.

Pavage: Toll for the upkeep of roads.

Peruke: Also periwig, for men in the 17th and 18th centuries.

Piccage: Toll for breaking ground to set up stalls.

Pontage: Toll for the upkeep of bridges.

Purpresture: Encroachment of Crown lands. Liable to a fine.

Reeve: A man elected by his fellows as organiser of the group. Also as spokesman in any negotiations with the Lord of the Manor.

Scot and Lot: Payments by town dwellers for borough facilities — the forerunner of the present day rates.

Selion: A cultivated strip in an open field consisting of ridge and furrow in some grass fields today.

Seize: A freeholder was said to be seized of his land if he possessed it.

Shire: Pre-Norman division of Old English Kingdom of Provinces. Mercia divided in 10th century.

Silica Sand: A rough grained soil containing dioxide of silicon used in making glass, ceramics etc.

Stallage: Toll for pitching stalls in fairs and markets without breaking ground.

Stipendiary: Receiving a fixed salary.

Stratum: A distinct layer of rock. Strata — layers.

Syncline: A downward fold of stratified rock.

Terracotta: The clay from which unglazed brownish-red earthenware is made.

Thegn/Thane: One who was part of the King's household or military supporter.

Tolls: Taxes paid on the spot for various purposes.

Turnpike: A barrier on a road which was only raised when the toll for the upkeep of the highway was paid.

Tundra: A treeless zone between the ice sheet and the timber line. The subsoil is permanently frozen.

Victualler: Licensed by J.P. under 1552 Alehouse Act.

Virgate: A quarter of a hide. Normally about thirty acres.

BIBLIOGRAPHY

Albert, W., *The Turnpike Road System in England* (1972).

Anderson, J. C., *Shropshire, The Early History and Antiquities* (1972).

Barrow, C. C., *A Short History of St Nicholas Church, Newport.*

Beard, J., C.B.E., *My Shropshire Days in Common Ways* (1900).

Beresford, M., *New Towns in The Middle Ages* (1967).

Briggs, A., *The Age of Improvement 1783-1867* (1959).

Codrington, T., *Roman Roads in Britain* (1905).

Collingwood, R. G. and Myers, J. N. L., *Roman Britain* (1932).

Copeland, T., *Roads and their Traffic 1750–1850* (1968).

Cranage, Rev. D. H. S., *The Churches of Shropshire* (1905).

Darby, H. C. and Terret, I. B. (eds.), *The Domesday Geography of Midland England* (1954).

Directories: *Barfoot and Wilkes* (1789); *Pigott* (1822); *Robson's* (1840); *Slaters* (1850, 1868); *Post Office* (1856, 1870); *Kelly's* (1885, 1900, 1917, 1926, 1941).

Elliot, D. J., *Shropshire Clock and Watchmakers* (1979).

Eyton, R. W., *Antiquities of Shropshire* (vol. 8).

Farrow, W. J., *The Great Civil War in Shropshire* (1926).

Geological Survey of Britain (1928).

Hadfield, C., *The Canals of the West Midland* (1966).

Hoskins, W. G., *Fieldwork in History* (1983).

Houghton, Rev. W., *The Natural History of the Weald Moors.* Severn Valley Field Club.

Jackman, W. T., *The Development of Transport in Modern England* (1962).

Journal of The Shropshire Archaeological Society.

Journal of Transport, vol. 4 (November 1962).

Kirby, D. P., *The Making of Early England* (1961).

Lenton, J. H., *Methodism in Wellington* (1982).

Loch, J., *An Account of the Improvements of the Estate of the Marquess of Stafford* (1820).

Maitland, F. W., *Domesday Book and Beyond* (1960).

Page, R. I., *Life in Anglo-Saxon England* (1971).

Pevsner, N., *The Buildings of England: Shropshire* (1958).

Poole, A. L., *From Domesday Book to Magna Carta* (1955).

Rowley, T., *The Shropshire Landscape* (1972).

Smiles, S., *Lives of the Engineers*, vol. 1 (1968).

Twenlow, F. R., *The Battle of Bloreheath* (1912).

Trinder, Barrie, *A History of Shropshire* (1983).

Watts, W. W., *Shropshire, The Geography of the County* (1939).

Wells, A. K., *Outline of Historical Geology* (1959).

Wills, L. J., *The Palaeography of the Midlands* (1950).

Woods, W., *England in the Age of Chaucer.*

INDEX